Fingerspelling in American Sign Language

Brenda E. Cartwright and Suellen J. Bahleda

RID Press
Registry of Interpreters for the Deaf, Inc.
333 Commerce Street
Alexandria, VA 22314   USA
(703) 838-0030 V, (703) 838-0459 TTY, (703) 838-0454 Fax
www.rid.org

Registry of Interpreters for the Deaf, Inc.

The Registry of Interpreters for the Deaf, Inc. (RID) is the only national organization of professionals who provide sign language interpreting/transliterating services for Deaf and Hard of Hearing persons. Established in 1964 and incorporated in 1973, RID is a tax-exempt 501(c)(3) non-profit organization.

RID has worked diligently to provide the "three Q's of interpreting: Quantity, Qualifications, and Quality," namely, the RID Triad. RID's Triad is composed of

- Training for new and professional Interpreters through the Certification Maintenance Program (CMP)

- Continued certification through RID's National Testing System (NTS)

- Self-regulation through a national Ethical Practices System (EPS)

RID Press is a division of the Registry of Interpreters for the Deaf, Inc., 333 Commerce Street, Alexandria VA 22314, USA, (703) 838-0030 V, (703) 838-0459 TTY, (703) 838-0454 Fax.

Published 2002

Internet: www.rid.org

ISBN 0-916883-34-5

Printed in the United States of America

Contents

Authors' Note

This book is the result of more than ten years of development, experimentation, and collaboration. As faculty members in American Sign Language/Interpreter Programs, we developed this text to fulfill the need for fingerspelling curricula. Based on advances in linguistic knowledge of and insights into American Sign Language, approaches to fingerspelling instruction have evolved from letter-by-letter encoding and decoding to pattern and shape recognition of these elements.

Our instructional materials have grown to incorporate drills, expressive and receptive activities, information on lexical borrowing, and a number of evaluation methods. The mind-body connection has also been a topic of growing importance; therefore, we address the importance of a positive mindset when fingerspelling and the physical mechanics of the hand in relation to potential cumulative stress trauma.

Our goal is to create a practical, useful, and comprehensive approach to fingerspelling instruction. This process has energized and challenged us to evaluate our own instructional approaches and materials. We believe this book and its companion, *Numbering in American Sign Language*, capture that energy, and will support and enhance fingerspelling instruction across the spectrum, from beginning students to interpreters-in-training.

Our thanks to the students, workshop participants, and esteemed colleagues who provided testing grounds and invaluable feedback.

Brenda E. Cartwright, MS
CSC, CI and CT
Lansing Community College
Lansing, Michigan
BCartwright@lcc.edu

Suellen J. Bahleda, M.Ed.
CI and CT
University of Alaska Anchorage
Anchorage, Alaska
ansjb1@uaa.alaska.edu

Introduction

Fingerspelling, the *manual alphabet*, and *dactylology* are all terms used to describe the process of combining hand positions for individual letters of the alphabet to form words. On the surface, it is amazingly simple to learn the 26 shapes that comprise the American Sign Language (ASL) alphabet. Yet stringing those shapes together, both expressively and receptively, to create an understandable message, is perceived as one of the most frustrating aspects of ASL learning for adult learners. An informative, positive, and practical approach to fingerspelling instruction will allow students to view fingerspelling as an integral part of ASL learning, rather than an isolated component difficult to master.

The initial learning of and exposure to fingerspelling, and the ways in which students incorporate fingerspelling into practice, greatly impact students' attitude and ability to successfully use fingerspelling in ASL utterances. When the alphabet handshapes are learned in the order of the English alphabet, students can learn to spell and, to some extent, see fingerspelled information, but most often they continue to produce and decode with a letter-by-letter approach. Additionally, when students misuse fingerspelling as a stop-gap measure when they do not know a sign, they derail the template building necessary to recognize information fingerspelled to them.

This book provides a positive framework for teaching fingerspelling, with information and activities both expressive and receptive, aimed at providing relevant and enjoyable fingerspelling practice.

Unit One

❖ **Fingerspelling History**

❖ **Fingerspelling Usage**

❖ **Starting to Fingerspell**

❖ **Preventing Repetitive Motion Injury**

❖ **Classmate Roundtable Game**

Fingerspelling History

The manual alphabet used by American signers consists of 26 individual handshapes corresponding to letters of the English alphabet (see Appendix A), and has its historical roots in Spain. The handshapes of the manual alphabet were originally taken from a book of prayers written by a Franciscan monk, Melchor Yebra. Each letter of the alphabet had a prayer associated with it; if a monk was too ill to recite the prayer, he could indicate his prayer intent by making the corresponding handshape (Lane, 1984). Use of the handshapes to form whole words and messages evolved, allowing monks to communicate without violating their vows of silence (Schein, 1984). The concept of a handshape representation of letters of the alphabet was then borrowed for use in educating the deaf at the National Institution for Deaf-Mutes in Paris, where Laurent Clerc was a pupil and an instructor. In 1817, when he and Thomas Gallaudet established the American Asylum for the Education and Instruction of Deaf and Dumb Persons, in Hartford, Connecticut, fingerspelling was an integral component of signed language.

In the 1950s and 60s, the Rochester Method of educating deaf students required both teachers and students to speak English and fingerspell each word simultaneously. Everything from daily lessons to the school play was done this way.

While fingerspelling in other countries is not used in all sign languages to the same extent it is used in American Sign Language (ASL), most national sign languages have developed some kind of fingerspelled alphabet. One-handed or two-handed, most of these alphabets correspond to the alphabet of the spoken or written language used in that country.

Fingerspelling, as used in the United States, is a direct, letter-by-letter representation of English words. As an incorporated component of sign language communication, fingerspelling has various but specific uses within ASL.

Fingerspelling Usage

In American Sign Language, fingerspelling is used sparingly and specifically. It is important to recognize these uses and have them reflected in student practice. Once students learn how and why fingerspelling is used in American Sign Language, and practice using it expressively according to those precepts, their receptive ability will also be enhanced. Fingerspelled information will seem less random, instead, generally falling into specific category types.

The most common use of fingerspelling is for names. This includes:

- First and last names of people and pets:
  Donald Baxter, Terrell Johnson, Jing-Mei, Muffin, Champ, Squeaky
- Places:
  Maple Ave., Juarez, Arby's, Yosemite, Sears
- Book, movie, magazine, and television show titles:
  "Sign of Foul Play," "Beyond Silence," *Ebony*, "The West Wing"

A second use of fingerspelling is for technical terms and profession-bound words, such as vocabulary specific to a particular profession. This includes scientific, medical, and legal terminology, as well as other jargon associated with a particular profession. Examples include fistula, Xanex, goiter, escrow, blue midge, altimeter, and grout.

Fingerspelling is also used for a number of clarification purposes. It may be used to:

- Specify a particular word for a sign that may have many English synonyms:
  sign HOUSE + fingerspelled C-A-B-I-N
- Specify within a general category: sign CHOCOLATE + fingerspelled S-N-I-C-K-E-R-S
- Present a single concept in multiple modes, usually the sign followed by the fingerspelling: CAR C-A-R, FUN F-U-N, and DORM D-O-R-M.

Other specialized uses of fingerspelling (lexicalizing, acronyms, etc.) will be discussed in later sections.

Note: American Sign Language is a visual-gestural language rather than a written one. In order to discuss signs and fingerspelling, it has become standard practice to refer to a sign in writing by using all capital letters (CHOCOLATE) and to fingerspelling by all capital letters separated by hyphens (S-N-I-C-K-E-R-S).

Starting to Fingerspell

There are two aspects to fingerspelling: doing it yourself (expressive) and seeing and understanding someone else doing it (receptive.) Here are some beginning guidelines for expressive fingerspelling:

- Fingerspell words, not letters. As you fingerspell, think of the sound of the word (VIOLETS), not the letters (V,I,O,L,E,T,S). This will contribute to your rhythm, and to the receiver's ability to decode a whole shape, not just a string of letters. If you say the word as you fingerspell it, be sure to say it (and NOT the letters) *as* you are spelling it, not prior to beginning to spell it, nor afterwards, like an echo.

- As you spell, your hand may move slightly to the right (if you are right-handed; left, if you are left-handed) throughout the production of the word. Don't pile letters one on top of the other in the same space.

- Hold the last letter an additional beat to show completion, especially if another fingerspelled item follows it.

- Fingerspelling is not a sanctioned Olympic event; there are no medals for speed. Clarity, and developing a smooth, consistent rhythm or cadence within your whole signed message, is the key.

- Practice the shape of your first and last name until you can do it smoothly. This is usually the first thing you have to spell when you meet a Deaf person, and it's a relief to cross that hurdle without a mistake.

Preventing Repetitive Motion Injuries

American Sign Language and Interpreter Programs can play an important role in preventing repetitive motion injuries (Stewart et al, 1988). Just as athletes warm up, and increase their stamina in increments, so should signers and interpreters. Students should be encouraged to do warm-up stretches before fingerspelling practice.

The following warm-up stretches work to reduce the amount of stress the hand, wrist, arm, and shoulder receive while fingerspelling and signing. Each class session should begin with a variety of warm-ups to limit potential cumulative trauma disorders. Warm-up stretches may be selected from the following:

Shoulder Shrugs: Slowly raise and drop shoulders several times.

The Swan Dive: Slowly stretch arms above your head until they meet, palms together. Gently lower them to shoulder level, palms up. Repeat.

Finger Lifts: Place hand palm down on a table or flat surface and slowly raise and lower each finger. Repeat with the other hand.

Full Arm Stretch: Hold arm out parallel to the floor, palm down. Lock elbow. Raise your hand so the fingertips point to the ceiling. With the other hand, gently press the raised fingers back toward your body, for a five-count. Alternate with the other hand and repeat twice.

Palm Press: Press palms together in front of your body. Keeping your elbows high, use your right palm to gently and slowly push the left palm backwards, from the wrist only, toward the left elbow. Slowly and gently, use the left palm to push the right palm backward, from the wrist only, toward the right elbow. Repeat several times.

The Frankenstein: With arms stretched out in front of you, palms down, slowly open and close hands, stretching the fingers apart as far as possible. Repeat several times.

Wrist Revolutions: With closed hands, slowly rotate wrists in toward each other several times. Then rotate wrists away from each other several times.

Classmate Roundtable Game

➤ **Suggested Activity:** Students sit in a circle, each student folds a piece of paper in half lengthwise and writes his or her name on it. Place the name "tents" in front of each person so all can see the others' names. The first person in the circle spells his or her name. The next person fingerspells the first person's name, and adds his or her own. The next person fingerspells the first two names, and adds his or her own. This continues around the room, until the first person has fingerspelled the names of the entire group.

After the first person has fingerspelled the names of everyone, all stand up and randomly move to a different seat, with or without the name "tents." Select one student to fingerspell the names of everyone in their new locations, going around the circle. This can be repeated several times, until everyone can confidently spell every classmate's name.

Unit Two

- ❖ **Warm-Up Exercises**
- ❖ **Fingerspelling Tips**
- ❖ **Seeing Shapes**
- ❖ **Fingerspelling Drills**
- ❖ **Developmental Shape Drills**
- ❖ **Easy Opposites**
- ❖ **Let's Get Personal**
- ❖ **Men's and Women's Names**

Warm-Up Exercises

Shoulder Shrugs: Slowly raise and drop shoulders several times.

The Swan Dive: Slowly stretch arms above your head until they meet, palms together. Gently lower them to shoulder level, palms up. Repeat.

Finger Lifts: Place hand palm down on a table or flat surface and slowly raise and lower each finger. Repeat with the other hand.

Full Arm Stretch: Hold arm out parallel to the floor, palm down. Lock elbow. Raise your hand so the fingertips point to the ceiling. With the other hand, gently press the raised fingers back toward your body, for a five-count. Alternate with the other hand and repeat twice.

Palm Press: Press palms together in front of your body. Keeping your elbows high, use your right palm to gently and slowly push the left palm backwards, from the wrist only, toward the left elbow. Slowly and gently, use the left palm to push the right palm backward, from the wrist only, toward the right elbow. Repeat several times.

The Frankenstein: With arms stretched out in front of you, palms down, slowly open and close hands, stretching the fingers apart as far as possible. Repeat several times.

Wrist Revolutions: With closed hands, slowly rotate wrists in toward each other several times. Then rotate wrists away from each other several times.

Fingerspelling Tips

Warm-up and stretch out before a practice or class session. Fingerspelling shouldn't hurt. If you start to feel discomfort or pain during practice, stop and stretch out again.

Relax. Fingerspelling occurs within natural signed communication. It should happen at the same signing pace and rhythm as the rest of your signed message. If you are signing and you tense up when you fingerspell, you break that rhythm. Release the tension in your fingers, wrist, elbow, and shoulder.

Becoming a good fingerspeller requires practice. Make sure your practice reflects appropriate fingerspelling use in American Sign Language, and that you incorporate the suggestions below. It is much easier to form good habits from the beginning than to break bad ones later.

Where Does My Hand Go When I Fingerspell?

- When you fingerspell, your palm should generally be out toward the receiver, not toward yourself. In group settings, it is not possible to direct your spelling to all receivers.

- Keep your elbow close to your waist; don't let it drift away from your body.

- Your hand should be in your general shoulder area. Research shows that Deaf people focus on the chin/throat area when reading signed communication, but still see the whole sign space. Your hand should not block your mouth, to allow for supplemental lipreading clarification and non-manual marker grammatical clues.

- If needed, you may initially hold your wrist or elbow when fingerspelling to prevent bouncing. This should be a steadying grasp, not a death grip! (See "relax," above.) This is used as a learning technique to develop good habits; it is not normally done when naturally signing.

Seeing Shapes

Receptive understanding of fingerspelling is a bit like Professor Harold Hill's "think" system in *The Music Man*. Part of understanding receptive fingerspelling is believing that you can understand it. Learning to see shapes as whole ideas and thoughts within a context may seem like an unfamiliar task in the beginning, but it is also a strategy we use for reading English — a strategy that was learned through practice. Below is a group of sentences that have a key word outlined only by the shape of the English letters of that word, integrated into a contextual sentence. Based on the shape of the letters as they appear in written English, and the sentence contexts, identify the missing word.

Note: This exercise is not meant to be fingerspelled, but only serves as a reminder that shape-based understanding is a skill you have in English. The developing goal is to transfer that skill and confidence to fingerspelling. (See Answer Key, page 104, in Appendix B)

1. A ☐☐☐☐ is king of the jungle.

2. The ☐☐☐☐☐, also of the cat family, is found in India.

3. An ☐☐☐☐☐☐☐ has a prehensile trunk.

4. A ☐☐☐☐☐ dislocates its jaw to swallow prey.

5. A ☐☐☐☐☐ is adept at swinging from branches.

6. A grizzly ☐☐☐☐ hibernates in winter.

7. Take the groceries to the ☐☐☐☐☐☐.

8. Put candles on the table in the ☐☐☐☐☐ ☐☐☐☐.

9. I bought bunk beds for the ☐☐☐☐☐☐.

10. The ☐☐☐☐ was infested with squirrels.

11. The ☐☐☐☐☐☐☐ was converted into a rec room.

12. We have a big screen TV in the ☐☐☐☐☐ ☐☐☐☐.

Fingerspelling Drills

Fingerspelling drills meet a number of practice goals. These include the following:

- Fingerspelling practice can be physically demanding. Drills can be used to increase stamina. Remember to do warm-up exercises before beginning fingerspelling practice.

- Drills reinforce shape-based practice rather than letter-by-letter encoding and decoding.

- Drills create an opportunity to feel and to see how variations in production may occur based on the letters that precede or follow another. An "e" preceded by an "r" and followed by an "n" may be produced differently than one preceded by a "b" and followed by an "s."

- Drills assist in the development of rhythm and cadence.

The following drills develop and expand different shape combinations into increasingly longer words.

Developmental Shape Drills

or	at	av	as
corn	bat	ave	ast
scorn	bath	rave	cast
acorn	bathroom	brave	caste
acorns			castle

ic	if	ow	ow
hic	lif	own	row
hick	Cliff	low	crow
chicken	Clifford	clown	scarecrow
hickey			

ur	an	as	or
cur	Dan	ash	Ora
curt	dance	Asher	orate
curtain	Dancer	Dasher	decorate

di	ag	ap	ap
dis	rag	nap	cap
disc	drag	snap	cape
disco	dragon	snapdragon	escape
discover			

fe	am	or	en
fee	lam	for	end
feed	lame	fore	friend
feeds	flame	forest	friendly
feeder	flames	forecast	
feeders			

in	en	os	ow
fin	den	ost	low
fine	dens	host	flow
fined	garden	ghost	flower
defined	gardens		flowers

Developmental Shape Drills (continued)

ag	ac	ro	ai
age	ace	row	air
page	pace	grow	airs
pager	space	growth	stairs
pagers	spacer		
ol	ar	ad	il
old	ear	had	oil
cold	hear	shad	roil
scold	heart	shady	broil
	hearth	shadow	broiler
am	ra	pa	at
cam	ran	par	rat
came	rang	pare	rate
camel	range	parent	irate
camels	orange	spare	pirate
	ranger		
	Granger		
in	ri	ic	ip
pin	rim	ice	pip
pine	grim	rice	pipe
spine	pilgrim	price	pipes
lupine	grime		bagpipes
lupines			
il	bo	ro	ir
ail	boa	row	air
rail	boar	brow	lair
Braille	board	brown	flair
	boarder	brownie	Blair
el	wa	in	se
eel	war	kin	sea
reel	ward	skin	seas
creel	warden	skinny	season
	reward	kind	seasons
		kinder	seasoning
		kindergarten	

Easy Opposites

➤ **Suggested Activity:** This activity can be used in several ways:

- As expressive and receptive practice, flash cards can be made with the following word pairs. Student partners can fingerspell one of the paired words, and the partner spells the opposite back.
- As receptive practice only, the instructor spells one of the words, and students individually write the opposite on a piece of paper.
- As a relay game, the instructor divides the class into teams. One person from each team goes to the blackboard, ready to write. The instructor fingerspells a word and the first student to correctly write the opposite on the board wins a point for his or her team. Play to 10 or 15 points.

stand/sit	high/low	good/bad
above/below	near/far	hot/cold
remember/forget	mother/father	ride/walk
never/always	add/subtract	spicy/bland
empty/full	over/under	wet/dry
poor/rich	front/back	alive/dead
less/more	young/old	top/bottom
before/after	new/old	dark/light
first/last	fast/slow	quiet/noisy
south/north	come/go	tight/loose
east/west	long/short	salt/pepper
give/take	push/pull	black/white
dirty/clean	thick/thin	few/many
day/night	play/work	left/right
cold/hot	open/close	man/woman
big/small	buy/sell	hard/soft
laugh/cry	short/tall	cheap/expensive

Let's Get Personal

➤ **Suggested Activity:** With a partner, share the following information. Answers can be factual or invented. Be sure to use appropriate ASL structure and grammatical features for your answers.

1. **Basic introduction:**
   Your name?
   Employer?
   Where were you born?   '
   What month were you born?

2. **About your family:**
   Parents' names?
   Siblings' names?
   Pets' names?
   Favorite aunt or uncle's name?

3. **Favorite things:**
   Book?
   Car you would most like to own?
   Movie?
   Thing to eat?

Men's and Women's Names

➤ **Suggested Activity:** Divide into pairs. One partner uses List A and the other uses List B. Alternating, one fingerspells a name from List A; the partner says the name and then fingerspells a name from List B.

Women's Names

A.	B.
Abby	Lena
Robin	Sandra
Kameko	Cathy
Denise	Amy
Gail	Ashley
Chloe	Dolores
Betty	Adrian
Vicky	Lani
Jill	Eileen
Heidi	Tammy
Esther	Marie
Ebony	Gabrielle
Agnes	Inez
Wendy	Tanisha
Janet	Molly
Meg	Aileen
Ingrid	Yoshiko
Emma	Kelsey
Olivia	Alice
Faith	Helen
Phoebe	Chelsea
Amber	Valerie
Theresa	Natalie
Dorothy	Consuelo
Colleen	Michelle

Men's Names

A.	B.
Ross	Isaac
Seth	Dennis
Doug	Norman
Ben	Jeremy
Chris	Yoshi
Will	Karl
Stan	Harry
Paul	Drew
Owen	Todd
Erique	Tony
James	Steve
Rick	Brad
Brett	Gary
Scott	Ryan
Jeff	Evander
Roger	Bill
Caleb	Tim
Quinn	Jose
Justin	Russell
Mario	Alex
Floyd	Wayne
Ron	Toby
Jacob	Michael
Bronson	Reuben
Yoshiro	Jason

Men's and Women's Names (continued)

Men's Names		Women's Names	
A.	**B.**	**A.**	**B.**
Tom	Adam	Tracy	Grace
Gene	Sam	Erica	Samantha
Andy	Don	Brooke	Leigh
David	Greg	Carolyn	Alexi
Peter	Phillip	Edith	Shawna
Neil	Luke	Melissa	Caitlin
Lee	Brian	Patricia	Alyssa
Sean	Dale	Hannah	Lucy
Bobby	Eddie	Reiko	Gwen
Chad	Dean	Rebecca	Kristi
Aaron	Lewis	Julia	Cindy
Kyle	Dan	Josie	Dora
Ray	Mark	Alicia	Holly
Ian	Henry	Andrea	Mandy
Randy	Perry	Adele	Della
Matthew	Barry	Sara	Allison
Blair	Kareem	Ann	Beth
Allen	Tyler	Leslie	Debbie
Troy	Quentin	Zoe	Sherry
Joe	Warren	Barbara	Stephanie
Glenn	Zachary	Dana	Kerry
Casey	Hans	Jennifer	Rachel
Nathan	Pablo	Paige	Nichole
John	Stuart	Veronica	Jessica
Tanner	Patrick	Nakiya	Keisha
Gordon	Yuri	Lily	Peggy
Luis	Cody	Oksana	Conchita
Hakeem	Oliver	Diana	Whitney
Charles	Micah	Gillian	Lisa
Sven	Martin	Danielle	Penny
Ahmed	Rafael	Constance	Maude
Jeremy	Darrell	Janice	Linda
Dillon	Cole	Lee	Daria
Terry	Nicholas	Juanita	Sybil
Richard	Dennis	Naomi	Estelle

Unit Three

* **Warm-Up Exercises**
* **Developmental Shape Drills**
* **Making Clozure**
* **The 50 States**
* **Geography Bowl**

Warm-Up Exercises

Shoulder Shrugs: Slowly raise and drop shoulders several times.

The Swan Dive: Slowly stretch arms above your head until they meet, palms together. Gently lower them to shoulder level, palms up. Repeat.

Finger Lifts: Place hand palm down on a table or flat surface and slowly raise and lower each finger. Repeat with the other hand.

Full Arm Stretch: Hold arm out parallel to the floor, palm down. Lock elbow. Raise your hand so the fingertips point to the ceiling. With the other hand, gently press the raised fingers back toward your body, for a five-count. Alternate with the other hand and repeat twice.

Palm Press: Press palms together in front of your body. Keeping your elbows high, use your right palm to gently and slowly push the left palm backwards, from the wrist only, toward the left elbow. Slowly and gently, use the left palm to push the right palm backward, from the wrist only, toward the right elbow. Repeat several times.

The Frankenstein: With arms stretched out in front of you, palms down, slowly open and close hands, stretching the fingers apart as far as possible. Repeat several times.

Wrist Revolutions: With closed hands, slowly rotate wrists in toward each other several times. Then rotate wrists away from each other several times.

Developmental Shape Drills

li	si	ow	ow
lid	sin	owl	low
slid	sing	bowl	blow
slide	single	bowler	blower
slider	singer		
	Bassinger		

ow	in	lk	ut
now	tin	ilk	out
snow	ting	silk	pout
snowblower	tingle	silken	spout
	sting	silky	rout
	stinger		sprout

or	oy	ar	us
ore	Roy	car	use
tore	Troy	scar	muse
store	destroy	Oscar	museum
stores	destroyer		

ta	at	te	in
tab	cat	tea	win
table	scat	tease	wine
tablet	scatter	teaser	twine
stab			entwine
stable			

at	ip	al	aw
eat	rip	ale	law
heat	trip	hale	slaw
wheat	ripe	whale	coleslaw
heater	tripe	whales	
cheat	stripe	whaler	
cheater	strip		
	stripper		

Developmental Shape Drills (continued)

af	am	ar	ar
aft	amp	car	har
after	camp	Cara	char
afternoon	scamp	caraway	Charles
rafter	scampi		Charleston

as	ar	an	an
ask	ark	can	and
bask	park	cant	sand
basket	spark	canter	Sandy
basketball	Sparky	Canterbury	sandal

ug	id	be	ay
rug	rid	bee	lay
drug	ride	bees	clay
druggist	bride	beeswax	Clayton
drugstore	bridegroom		Barclay

op	ar	el	or
hop	art	eel	ord
hopper	dart	heel	word
grasshopper	Darth	wheel	sword
chop	Dartmouth	wheelchair	swordfish
chopper			
shop			
shopper			

ow	en	aw	ac
low	end	awn	ack
slow	tend	pawn	lack
slowpoke	tender	awning	black
	tenderfoot	pawning	blackberry
		yawn	
		yawning	

ol	an	on	ma
old	han	one	mas
gold	Chan	hone	mast
goldfish	Chang	phone	master
	change	earphone	masterpiece
	exchange		

Making Clozure

Beginning fingerspellers need to develop confidence in their ability to decode complete messages from incomplete information — to process information without comprehending "all the letters," even though they are given. This process is called "clozure." The following activity is designed to build confidence that it is possible to comprehend the meaning in a word-string without seeing each and every component, and even without context. The key is to think *words*, not letters. This exercise can be done either with overhead transparencies or flashcards. (See Answer Key, page 105, in Appendix B.)

NOTE: This exercise is not meant to be fingerspelled.

QUSIMDO	RCHL	LZBTH
BCTRA	KLMZO	LINGNI
SPRGTN	FLGFF	PNICLN
CDRLLA	CLTN	TMTHY
TZMNA	MLBRNE	HNRY
LXNTN	BFLO	SHKSPR
CHYNE	JRY	ZBR
LZRD	AMRLLO	ANDRSN
CPNHGN	BJNG	SWZKPF
PTLND	JSCA	DNLD
CRWFD	BKWRM	CRLYN
OLV GRDN	JC PNY	CLVLND
BNJMN	DFODL	BSTN
MRGRT	DTH VDR	HLYWD
SPRGFLD	HNKKH	LTHUNA
RKFLR	STPHN	TSCNY
LVRPL	NDLPNT	MCHL
BRBRA	PNSTTA	NW ZLND

The 50 States

American Sign Language has a number of approaches to identifying the 50 states. A combination of signs from older post office designations, 2-, 3-, and 4-letter postal abbreviations, and spelling the entire name are used. Some state signs have fallen into disfavor, while others are emerging. For example, signers in the West have developed an initialized sign for Oregon, coming from the shoulder, as in the sign for "Washington." Oregon signers, in the ongoing quest to be seen as an entity separate from Washington, prefer to sign a shaken "O" in the neutral sign space. The map below identifies the most common standard approach for each state, although regional and generational variations may be found.

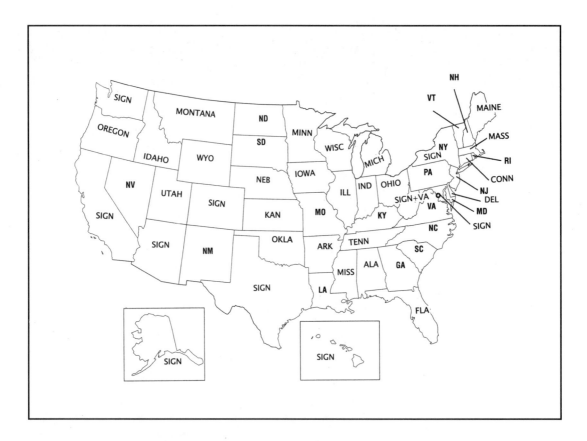

Alaska, Arizona, California, Colorado, Hawaii, New York, Texas, Washington, Washington D.C., and West Virginia, have nationally accepted signs.

Geography Bowl

➤ **Suggested Activity:** In pairs, take turns asking and answering the following questions related to U.S. geography. (See Answer Key, page 106, in Appendix B.)

1. Which state is known as "The Last Frontier"?

2. Name the five Great Lakes.

3. Name seven states that border the Atlantic Ocean.

4. Name three states that border the Pacific Ocean.

5. Which two mountain states are shaped like squares?

6. Which four states border Mexico?

7. Name five states that border Canada.

8. Which state is located on both the Gulf of Mexico and the Atlantic Ocean?

9. Name three of the Hawaiian Islands.

10. Which state is shaped like a boot?

11. Which state is surrounded by fresh water lakes?

12. What is the capital of Indiana?

13. Name four of the seven states that border Kentucky.

14. What state is known as "the Cornhusker State"?

15. Name three of the four state capitals with the word "City" in their names.

Unit Four

- ❖ **Warm-Up Exercises**
- ❖ **Developmental Shape Drills**
- ❖ **What Do I Do If I Miss the Fingerspelling?**
- ❖ **Making Clozure with Context**
- ❖ **Making a Whole from Parts**
- ❖ **Double Letters**
- ❖ **Words Per Minute**

Warm-Up Exercises

Shoulder Shrugs: Slowly raise and drop shoulders several times.

The Swan Dive: Slowly stretch arms above your head until they meet, palms together. Gently lower them to shoulder level, palms up. Repeat.

Finger Lifts: Place hand palm down on a table or flat surface and slowly raise and lower each finger. Repeat with the other hand.

Full Arm Stretch: Hold arm out parallel to the floor, palm down. Lock elbow. Raise your hand so the fingertips point to the ceiling. With the other hand, gently press the raised fingers back toward your body, for a five-count. Alternate with the other hand and repeat twice.

Palm Press: Press palms together in front of your body. Keeping your elbows high, use your right palm to gently and slowly push the left palm backwards, from the wrist only, toward the left elbow. Slowly and gently, use the left palm to push the right palm backward, from the wrist only, toward the right elbow. Repeat several times.

The Frankenstein: With arms stretched out in front of you, palms down, slowly open and close hands, stretching the fingers apart as far as possible. Repeat several times.

Wrist Revolutions: With closed hands, slowly rotate wrists in toward each other several times. Then rotate wrists away from each other several times.

Developmental Shape Drills

il	en	en	ag
ill	men	len	age
kill	amen	lent	sage
skill	Ramen	polenta	message
skills	foramen		sausage
Catskills			

ev	pi	ew	ev
eve	pic	new	Eva
even	pice	newt	Evan
evens	spice	Newton	Evans
Stevens	hospice		

st	st	or	an
ast	ast	orn	ban
east	last	horn	urban
yeast	blast	thorn	turban
	fibroblast	Thornfield	

li	lo	lo	al
Liz	los	log	all
Liza	loss	slog	wall
lizard	gloss	Logan	wallow
blizzard	glossary	slogan	swallow

ar	at	ar	ay
arm	tat	arc	ray
warm	stat	arch	pray
swarm	status	parch	spray
		parchment	sprayer

al	il	li	an
gal	oil	lic	pan
gala	coil	lice	span
galaxy	recoil	Alice	spank
			Spanky

What Do I Do If I Miss the Fingerspelling?

Shifting the perspective from what you "missed" to what you *saw* can develop confidence and a positive mindset. If you know that fingerspelling happened, then you didn't *miss* anything. You *saw* fingerspelling happen. If you allow the whole fingerspelled information to happen, and begin an analysis based on what was seen, rather than what was missed, it not only reinforces a positive message, but leads to strategies to decode fingerspelling. Length of the fingerspelled item, beginning/ending shapes, shapes within the item, and contextual clues all are aspects of the analysis that can lead to successful decoding.

Be assured not every person understands every fingerspelled item produced by every signer. If information is integral to the message, it is often repeated, giving the receiver an opportunity to see it again and repeat the analysis/decoding process. The receiver may also make a value judgment that the fingerspelled information is incidental to the larger message; in a story about going on a group tour bus trip to an outlet mall, the name of a particular store the signer visited may not be vital to understanding the overall story.

Asking a speaker to slow down will not help. People have a natural conversational pace. Fingerspelling happens within that pace. Asking to slow down the fingerspelling disrupts the communication rhythm and feeds into a student's tendency to decode letter-by-letter.

Use all the clues available. Don't watch the hand of the signer, but instead focus on the face, where mouthing and other grammatical information might help with decoding.

Ask for clarification or repeats by identifying parts that were understood. If the receiver knows the fingerspelled piece was a professor's name, ask PROFESSOR NAME WHAT? or spell back what was understood (J-A-C-O-B-O-W...) This assures the signing partner that the receiver is understanding the overall message. In contrast, if the receiver signs SORRY I MISS PLEASE REPEAT, the signing partner is not sure exactly what has been missed, or how far back to go in the story.

Practice reading fingerspelling from angles other than face-to-face. Conversation can happen in a variety of group settings, so receivers may need to decode from different perspectives, depending on where he's standing or sitting in a group.

Making Clozure with Context

An important skill for receptive fingerspelling is learning to wait. Often, students interrupt a signer misspelling when they realize a fingerspelled element is in progress. They feel they weren't "ready" to catch the fingerspelling, that their eyes "missed" the beginning of the word and won't be able to catch up. In truth, if they allow the fingerspelled element to be completed AND wait for a few contextual signs to follow, they typically can piece together the fingerspelled part. It feels like a leap of faith, but it's really a positive strategy.

The following activity helps to develop prediction skills in addition to clozure skills. Prediction skills are used, based on the context of the conversation, to think ahead to what elements may be included. Then, if and when they are fingerspelled, they are comprehended in a snap, because the receiver expected it to show up sooner or later.

This leads to one other aspect of receptive fingerspelling: we see what we know. If the context is a subject students are familiar with, chances are, they will be able to successfully decode the fingerspelled content, based on knowledge of the subject. A basketball fan will read "pick and roll," "Hornets" and "Kareem Abdul-Jabar" without missing a beat, while a rock and roll fan will not blink at "Aerosmith", "Lalapalooza" and "Eddie Van Halen."

This activity builds on the exercise in Unit Three. Again, the incomplete words can be done on overhead transparencies or flashcards. The instructor may show students the context sentence, stopping before reaching the target word(s). Students then brainstorm predicted elements that could complete the sentence. The complete sentence is then shown, with the incomplete target word. Students should match their predictions to the target word to identify the correct answer.

Note: This is a developmental activity to identify English strategies that may be transferred to fingerspelling. This activity is not meant to be signed or fingerspelled. (See Answer Key, page 107, in Appendix B.)

1. To make a rich spaghetti sauce, you need tomatoes and plenty of RGNO.

2. The results of my biopsy showed the tumor to be BNGN.

3. My favorite Christmas candle scent is MLBRY.

4. Amanda's favorite Disney movie is LTL MRMD.

5. Tristan sent college applications to DRMTH, PRCTN and YLE.

6. For the French Club's final meeting, we ate at CHZ LUIS. I just had the French onion soup, but Lydia tried the ESCRGT.

7. When I was in Rome, I saw several works by MCLNGLO, including the STNE CHPL ceiling, and the PITA.

Making Clozure with Context (continued)

8. In Paris, I saw the GRGYL at Notre Dame and the FFL Tower.

9. Stephen King wrote one of my favorite books, GRN ML. It was made into a movie with TM HKS.

10. When we go out to eat, Jeff orders a PTRHSE steak. I usually order the FLT MGN.

11. Because Susan was afraid her boyfriend would become violent when they broke up, she got a RSTRNG RDR against him.

12. Bailey's favorite characters on Sesame Street are SCR and BG BRD.

13. At the amusement park, Terry and Cathy rode three rides, the RLR CSTR, the MRY G RND and the TLT WRL.

14. Chris decided to become a flight attendant for STHWST Airlines and moved to TCSN.

15. Because local doctors couldn't figure out what was wrong with her, Marie was sent first to the MYO CLNC, and then to the JHN HPKNS Medical Center.

16. Our third president, Thomas JFRSN, lived at MNTCLO, in Virginia.

17. When our dental HYGNST had a baby, we gave her a gift certificate to TRGT.

Making a Whole from Parts

➤ **Suggested Activity:** In small groups, brainstorm and fingerspell as many words as you can that contain the following shapes and are words that would be fingerspelled in American Sign Language.

Complete words can be made by using the shape in its entirety, or by using the letters within a larger word. Example: FREDDY, FLORENCE, and FIRESTARTER would be acceptable responses for FRE, but not FRIEND because there is a sign for it. The television program FRIENDS, however, would be acceptable because it is the title of a show.

FRE	THU
PRA	LUG
DAR	CLY
BIS	MET
HOC	NST
ALP	GOV
RIV	DCM
ADR	HBN
GRD	PST
VCY	SWL
CTH	ERN

Double Letters

Fingerspelled items that contain double letters are produced in a variety of ways. Which letter is being formed, where the letter appears in the word, and personal preference all contribute to these variations in production. The goal in double-letter production is to make it efficient, and to match the rhythm of the fingerspelling.

Some double letters are produced with a short, repeated contact movement. For example, in the name "Laura Redden Searing," the "d"s in Redden would be made by a small touch-release-touch of the thumb to the index finger.

Other double letters are produced by holding the letter shape and sliding it slightly to the right (for right-handed signers; to the left for left-handed signers). When fingerspelling "Tinkerbell," the "l" shape will be repeated as a slight slide. However, when fingerspelling "Phyllis," instead of the repeated "l"s being held and moved, the "l" shape will be repeated as a short, forward tap in place.

Practice producing double letters with the following:

William	Pickett	Greene	Pierre
Cassatt	Sellers	Kimmel	Thaddeus
Burr	Wittenberg	Sussex	Emma
Fillmore	Savannah	Agrippina	Crockett
cloissone	Eddie	Annapolis	Vermeer
Soong	Tipperary	Walla Walla	Flynn
Ferrari	Booth	Greeley	Tallahassee
Annie	Phillip	Rousseau	Kerry
Innsbruck	Steffens	Battle Creek	Hopper
Reed	Matthew	Harrison	Welles
Abruzzi	Keller	Hoover	Pyrenees
Pocatello	Hess	Billings	Camille
Gibbs	Hannibal	Jefferson	Mohammed
Tuscaloosa	Galilee	Appomattox	Ross
Sheffield	Kellogg	Barrow	Marshall
Chillicothe	Shannon	buzzard	Lorre
Holbrook	Dillon	Booker	Hermann
Cheyenne	Doolittle	Knossos	Cornwallis
Cassidy	Belle	Allen	buttress
Prussia	Cooperstown	Perry	Chappaquiddick
tweezers	Ellery	McConnell	Sagittarius
Tandoori chicken	jellyfish	pollen	satellite
Yellowstone	ricotta	Chunnel	Doppler
Holly	burrito	voodoo	Farrakhan
Isaac	shillelagh	antifreeze	fossil
Apollo	Challenger	mozzarella	cellulite

Words Per Minute

➤ **Suggested Activity:** Divide into pairs. One person holds the following list at eye level for the other. When the instructor gives a signal, the person not holding the list begins to fingerspell the words on the list. Each word must be fingerspelled clearly and completely (the person holding the list acts as an "accountability judge," ensuring each word is fingerspelled clearly and completely). At the end of one minute, the instructor gives a stop signal. Count how many words were fingerspelled. Switch roles, and repeat.

1.	RUN	21.	WITTY
2.	FUN	22.	CON
3.	BUN	23.	DON
4.	GUN	24.	NON
5.	NUN	25.	SON
6.	PUN	26.	TON
7.	SUN	27.	WON
8.	FUNNY	28.	CONE
9.	RUNNY	29.	DONE
10.	BUNNY	30.	NONE
11.	SUNNY	31.	TONE
12.	YOUNG	32.	GONE
13.	FIT	33.	HONE
14.	HIT	34.	LONE
15.	KIT	35.	DOG
16.	PIT	36.	FOG
17.	SIT	37.	HOG
18.	WIT	38.	JOG
19.	KITTY	39.	LOG
20.	PITY	40.	NOG

Unit Five

Warm-Up Exercises

Shoulder Shrugs: Slowly raise and drop shoulders several times.

The Swan Dive: Slowly stretch arms above your head until they meet, palms together. Gently lower them to shoulder level, palms up. Repeat.

Finger Lifts: Place hand palm down on a table or flat surface and slowly raise and lower each finger. Repeat with the other hand.

Full Arm Stretch: Hold arm out parallel to the floor, palm down. Lock elbow. Raise your hand so the fingertips point to the ceiling. With the other hand, gently press the raised fingers back toward your body, for a five-count. Alternate with the other hand and repeat twice.

Palm Press: Press palms together in front of your body. Keeping your elbows high, use your right palm to gently and slowly push the left palm backwards, from the wrist only, toward the left elbow. Slowly and gently, use the left palm to push the right palm backward, from the wrist only, toward the right elbow. Repeat several times.

The Frankenstein: With arms stretched out in front of you, palms down, slowly open and close hands, stretching the fingers apart as far as possible. Repeat several times.

Wrist Revolutions: With closed hands, slowly rotate wrists in toward each other several times. Then rotate wrists away from each other several times.

What Do I Do When I Make a Spelling Error?

If you make a spelling error, the easiest thing to do is just go on. Many times, your message will be understood, even when misspelled, based on the conversational context. Remember, it's not about letters, it's about *words*. If you do need to correct an error, indicate an error has been made (by facial expression, a hold/freeze of the hand accompanied by a headshake, or sign ERROR ME), and begin again. Don't "erase," slap your hand, etc. Your message is important, not your error.

Lexicalized Fingerspelling

Fingerspelled words that have undergone changes in the way they are produced and are now considered part of American Sign Language are called "lexicalized" or "loan signs" (Battison, 1978). These words were originally an exact, letter-by-letter borrowing from English that have been adapted and adopted by the Deaf community to enrich and expand the lexicon of ASL. These lexicalized fingerspelled words have been adapted in a number of ways: through changes in handshape, palm orientation, location, or movement; through combining letters; or by using both hands in the production. Additionally, some or all of the middle letters may be less articulated or "folded" into other production factors (palm orientation, location, and movement)

Common lexicalized three-letter words:

TOY	BUT	BUS	GAS	FAX
JOB	OFF	DOG	WOW	
WHO	FIX	ASK	HOW	
YES	CAR	BUG	OUT	

Common lexicalized four-letter words:

BURN	SALE	EASY	NEWS
BUSY	WILL	COOL	QUIZ
WHEN	HURT	CLUB	BANK
WHAT	SURE	SOON	

Common lexicalized five-letter words:

EARLY	FRESH	WOULD
SORRY	SISSY	SILLY

Lexicalized Fingerspelling (continued)

Additional lexicalized fingerspellings in American Sign Language:

DR	NO	DO	OK
EMAIL	IF	OH	HA
BACK	ALL	ON	STYLE
FUN	OWN	EX (spouse)	OR
GO	WELL	SEX	TV
RENT	VAN	CHECK	BAG
SICK	FLU	CUT	FOOT
HAIR	ROOF	CONDO	PIZZA
BOMB	STIFF	USED	SAFE
SO	NAIL	CASH	

American Sign Language also uses a number of fingerspelled abbreviations for lexical items. The following is a sampling:

TB (too bad)	NG (no good)	BS (bullshit)	KO (knocked out)
TF (task force)	PW (password)	NL (newsletter)	WC (worker's comp)
REF (refrigerator)	APT (apartment)	SEC (second)	BBQ (barbeque)
AC (air conditioner)	ID (identification)	OT (overtime)	HS (high school)
CHEV (Chevrolet)	SW (station wagon)	VW (Volkswagon)	PLY (Plymouth)
LB (pounds)	OZ (ounces)	CO (company)	VEG (vegetables)
REG (regular)	DEPT (department)	CHOL (cholesterol)	
VR (Vocational Rehabilitation)			

Developmental Shape Drills

ic	pr	ou	et
ick	pro	out	het
wick	prow	pout	Chet
wicker	prowl	spout	sachet
ai	ar	br	pa
ain	arp	bra	par
aint	harp	bran	park
taint	sharp	brand	spark
paint	Tharp	brandy	sparkle
saint	harpoon		
nk	iv	as	ea
ink	liv	asp	pea
link	live	rasp	pear
slink	olive	grasp	pearl
Slinky	Palmolive	raspberry	spear
am	av	ri	an
ram	ave	rip	lan
ramp	have	ripe	land
cramp	shave	tripe	Lando
crampon	shaver	stripe	Orlando
ac	im	ar	tr
ace	imp	ark	tra
race	limp	lark	trap
trace	blimp	Clark	strap
tracer	Blimpee's	Clarke	trapeze
ma	ge	pi	cu
Max	Gen	pit	cur
Maxi	Gene	spit	Curt
Maxine	Eugene	spite	Curtis
		respite	

Developmental Shape Drills (continued)

iv	in	ce	lo
ive	vin	cen	lop
live	vince	cent	lope
liver	Vincent	centaur	slope
Liverpool			elope

ar	le	we	af
bar	lex	wee	aft
Barb	Alex	weed	raft
Barbara	Alexander	tweed	craft
			Rafter

un	op	da	ru
lun	hop	Dan	dru
Lunt	chop	Dani	drum
blunt	chopper	Danish	redrum

be	gi	hu	ar
Ben	gin	hum	art
bent	gins	hump	wart
Benton	ginseng	chump	wartz
			Schwartz

ki	vi	wa	ax
Kim	avi	wan	tax
Kimber	ravi	swan	taxi
Kimberly	gravity	swans	taxidermy
		Swanson	

ze	ot	in	ad
aze	cot	tin	rad
maze	Scot	tint	Brad
amaze	Scott	stint	Brady
	Scotty		

Let's Get Personal

➤ **Suggested Activity:** With a partner, share the following information. Answers can be factual or invented. Be sure to use appropriate ASL structure and grammatical features for your answers.

1. **Home Sweet Home:**
   What street do you live on?
   What kind of refrigerator do you have?
   What kind of shampoo is in the bathroom?
   What CD do you play most often?

2. **Couch Potato:**
   What's your favorite snack while watching TV?
   What program do you watch every week?
   Who is your favorite TV actor or actress?
   What station do you watch for local news?

3. **Favorite Foods:**
   What is your favorite candy bar?
   What is your favorite flavor of ice cream?
   What is your favorite kind of cheese?
   What is your favorite restaurant?

States East of the Mississippi

➤ **Suggested Activity:** Arrange the class into a circle. The first student must give the appropriate sign, fingerspelling, or abbreviation for a state east of the Mississippi River. The next student must give another. A student is "out" if s/he gives the incorrect sign, fingerspelling, or abbreviation; repeats an already given state; or names a state west of the Mississippi River (See Answer Key, page 109, in Appendix B).

Unit Six

- ❖ **Warm-Up Exercises**
- ❖ **Fingerspelling Drills**
- ❖ **Which Ones?**

Warm-Up Exercises

Shoulder Shrugs: Slowly raise and drop shoulders several times.

The Swan Dive: Slowly stretch arms above your head until they meet, palms together. Gently lower them to shoulder level, palms up. Repeat.

Finger Lifts: Place hand palm down on a table or flat surface and slowly raise and lower each finger. Repeat with the other hand.

Full Arm Stretch: Hold arm out parallel to the floor, palm down. Lock elbow. Raise your hand so the fingertips point to the ceiling. With the other hand, gently press the raised fingers back toward your body, for a five-count. Alternate with the other hand and repeat twice.

Palm Press: Press palms together in front of your body. Keeping your elbows high, use your right palm to gently and slowly push the left palm backwards, from the wrist only, toward the left elbow. Slowly and gently, use the left palm to push the right palm backward, from the wrist only, toward the right elbow. Repeat several times.

The Frankenstein: With arms stretched out in front of you, palms down, slowly open and close hands, stretching the fingers apart as far as possible. Repeat several times.

Wrist Revolutions: With closed hands, slowly rotate wrists in toward each other several times. Then rotate wrists away from each other several times.

Fingerspelling Drills

As a reminder, fingerspelling drills meet a number of practice goals. These include the following:

- Fingerspelling practice can be physically demanding. Drills can be used to build up and increase stamina. Remember to do warm-up exercises before beginning fingerspelling practice.

- Drills reinforce shape-based practice rather than letter-by-letter encoding and decoding.

- Drills create an opportunity to feel and to see how variations in production may occur based on the letters that precede or follow another. An "e" preceded by an "r" and followed by an "n" may be produced differently than one preceded by a "b" and followed by an "s."

- Drills assist in the development of rhythm and cadence.

The drills in the previous units developed and expanded different shape combinations into increasingly longer words. In the units that follow, there are two different types of drills, which build on the practice introduced with earlier drills. Some drills incorporate a specific shape into the beginning, middle, or end of words. Some expand a shape, which may appear in the beginning, middle, or end of words, into increasingly longer words.

Leading Shape UN

Unalaska
unaneled
UNESCO
Unger
Unitarian
Universal Studios
Underground railway

undertow
undine
unicorn
Union City
Una
United Arab Emirates

ungulate
UNICEF
underworld
unsaturated
unguent

Untermeyer
unction
undecagon
underdog

Embedded Shape UN

dung
skunk
thunder
Lunden
Bunyan
Bunche
tuna
dunce
Chunnel
Funt
Munson
Kung Fu
junta
Bunsen
pound
Dunston
Punky Brewster
juniper
rune

funnel
bunt
dune
cummerbund
dungeon
prune
Gunther
nunchuck
Bunker Hill
bundt
Punjab
Edmund
conundrum
Runnymede
sauna
Punxsutawney
Norton Sound
Tunney
bungalow

fungus
Nunn
Dunne
Gunga Din
gunnysack
Munising
Bethune
Runser
brunch
tunic
sundae
cuneiform
fundus
Sun Yat-Sen
Muncie
Jung
Dungeness
Runyan
Huntley

punctuation
SUNY
tunnel
jungle
Munsters
tundra
lunar
tungsten
June
Hunter
Gunnar
Tunisia
Duncan
Munich
fungi
immunity
shunt
Gunnison

Ending Shape UN

noun
Cajun

Cancun
pronoun

faun
Bull Run

stun gun

Mixed Shape RO

roa	rob	roc	roc
roan	Robin	Rock	broccoli
roach	Robbins	Rocker	crocodile
cockroach	Robinson	Rockefeller	Rochelle
roadrunner	Robert	Rockette	proctor
Roanoke	robot	Rockwell	rococo
Broad Street	strobe	crock	
Broadway	carob	Rockne	
	fibroblast		

rod	rog	roi	rok
rodeo	grog	android	stroke
Rodney	troglodyte	asteroid	Roker
Roddy	Roger	steroid	Croker
Rodman	Rogers	Detroit	Brokaw
Rodin	Roget	introit	Broken Arrow
Frodo	Rogaine	groin	
		broil	
		Troilus	

rol	rol	rom	rom
troll	Rolfe	Rome	Strom
trolley	Tyrol	Romeo	Bromley
Rollie	Carol	Romero	bromide
Rollins	Carolyn	Romania	chrome
Roland	Harold	romaine	chromosome
Rolaids	Tootsie Roll	dromedary	Cromwell

ron	ron	roo	rop
drone	Ronald	rook	Roper
Peron	saffron	Brooke	tropical
Cameron	Cronkite	Brooklyn	propeller
Sharon	bronze	Roosevelt	gum drop
Calderon	irony	DeGroot	
Tyrone	coroner	kangaroo	

Mixed Shape RO (continued)

ros	ros	Gross	rou
Rosa	Rosco	Roth	Moulin Rouge
rosary	Roscommon	Rothchild	Proust
rosacea	rot	Rotterdam	Rousseau
Rose	Rossetti	Globetrotters	Rouen
Rosemary	Roswell	rottweiler	roulette
Ambrose	Crosby	rotisserie	Farouk
Melrose Place	Roslyn	rotunda	
Rosecrans			

rov	row	row	rox
Rover	Rowe	Turrow	Roxy
Grover	Crowe	Farrow	proxy
Garden Grove	Rowan	Barrow	peroxide
grovel	Rowena	Paltrow	Roxanne
Petrov	Rowley	Kudrow	Roxbury
		marrow	

roy	roz
Troy	Prozac
Elroy	
LeRoy	
Conroy	
Gilroy	
Viceroy	
Ackroyd	

Which Ones?

➤ **Suggested Activity:** Instructor fingerspells two words from each of the following groups. Students must place a check mark next to the selected items.

_____ Tommy	_____ Mark	_____ Donny
_____ Tammy	_____ Mike	_____ Wendy
_____ Timmy	_____ Nike	_____ Danny
_____ Sammy	_____ Mack	_____ Fanny

_____ Rose	_____ Terry	_____ Erin
_____ Rosa	_____ Barry	_____ Eric
_____ Ross	_____ Larry	_____ Erica
_____ Gross	_____ Harry	_____ Rick

_____ rodeo	_____ Rome	_____ Troy
_____ Roddy	_____ Romero	_____ Elroy
_____ Rodney	_____ Roman	_____ LeRoy
_____ Rodman	_____ Romania	_____ Conroy
_____ Rodin	_____ romaine	_____ Gilroy

_____ Turrow	_____ Esther	_____ Carl
_____ Farrow	_____ Hester	_____ Carla
_____ Barrow	_____ Chester	_____ Carol
_____ Marrow	_____ Heston	_____ Clara
_____ Paltrow	_____ Hesson	_____ Clare

▶ Unit Seven

- ❖ **Warm-Up Exercises**
- ❖ **Developmental Shape Drills**
- ❖ **Let's Get Personal**
- ❖ **Getting Creative**

Warm-Up Exercises

Shoulder Shrugs: Slowly raise and drop shoulders several times.

The Swan Dive: Slowly stretch arms above your head until they meet, palms together. Gently lower them to shoulder level, palms up. Repeat.

Finger Lifts: Place hand palm down on a table or flat surface and slowly raise and lower each finger. Repeat with the other hand.

Full Arm Stretch: Hold arm out parallel to the floor, palm down. Lock elbow. Raise your hand so the fingertips point to the ceiling. With the other hand, gently press the raised fingers back toward your body, for a five-count. Alternate with the other hand and repeat twice.

Palm Press: Press palms together in front of your body. Keeping your elbows high, use your right palm to gently and slowly push the left palm backwards, from the wrist only, toward the left elbow. Slowly and gently, use the left palm to push the right palm backward, from the wrist only, toward the right elbow. Repeat several times.

The Frankenstein: With arms stretched out in front of you, palms down, slowly open and close hands, stretching the fingers apart as far as possible. Repeat several times.

Wrist Revolutions: With closed hands, slowly rotate wrists in toward each other several times. Then rotate wrists away from each other several times.

Drill Shape EL

ael	bel	bel	bel
Disraeli	Belle	Belinda	beluga
Israel	Annibelle	Belize	Belmont
Raphael	Belloc	Bellingham	Belvedere
	Bellow	Belgium	Mabel
	Bellini	Belgrade	Babel
	Belladonna		

cel	cel	del	del
cello	Celt	Dell	Delphi
cellophane	Celtics	Rondell	delphinium
cellulose	Celeste	Handel	Delhi
cellulite	Celestine	Mandel	Delilah
Cellini	Celia	Delta	Delmonico
	Celine	deltoid	Delacroix
	celery		

eel	fel	gel	hel
creel	Felix	gelatin	Helen
Tarheel	Felicity	gelato	Helena
Steele	Felipe	gelding	Helms
Neely	Feldman	Nigel	Hellman
	feldspar	Hufnagel	Heller
	Rumsfeld		Shelley
	felt		Chelsea
	falafel		
	Rockefeller		

hel	iel	jel	kel
helix	Ariel	jelly bean	Kelly
helium	Daniels	jellyfish	Keller
Helga	Teniel	Jell-O	Kellogg
Helsinki	glockenspiel		kelp
Phelps	Spielberg		Kelsey
mohel			sheckel
			Siskel
			Skelton

Drill Shape EL (continued)

mel	mel	nel	pel
Melinda	Melmac	Nellie	Pele
Melissa	Mellon	Nellis	pelvis
Melba	melanoma	Nelson	pelican
Melbourne	Melrose Park	Rosnel	spelunker
Melville	Hummel	fennel	Peloponnesian War
Melvin	caramel	kennel	
Hamel			

rel	sel	tel	uel
Jacques Brel	Tinseltown	Mostel	gruel
Prell	Selma	hostel	Cruella
Sorrell	Selznick	Telemundo	
Darrell	Alka Seltzer	Tel Aviv	
morel	Hansel	Telemann	
trellis	mussel		
relish	Seldom Seen Slim		
relay			

vel	wel	yel	zel
velma	Welsh	Yellowstone	Zelda
velcro	Welty	Yeltsin	Zelig
veld	Wellington		Denzel
vellum	Wellesley		mozel tov
velour	welterweight		
National Velvet	Lewellyn		
Velveteen Rabbit	Welk		
Marvel Comics			

Leading Shape AR

Arnold	Arden	armadillo	Aryan
Araxa	Arcadia	Armenia	Argentina
Ares	Ariel	ark	Aruba
Arsenio	arachnid	Artesia	Arapaho
Artemis	archipelago	Aragon	argyle
Ararat	archeology	arsenic	Arafat
areola	Archibald	arroyo	Arabia
Arc de Triomphe	Armageddon	Arlington	Aristotle

Embedded Shape AR

Sarajevo	garbanzo	varicose	Niagara Falls
Sarah	Harvard	Tarzan	Sahara
Marx	Aaron	paradiddle	Jakarta
carnation	ovary	narwhal	Darlene
Parcheesi	Earl	garlic	carcinoma
Parker	Ward	Barry	Jared
Pearce	baroque	caribou	notary
Barcelona	parasite	quarantine	Fargo
Karen	harlequin	marquis	Warren
Larry	maraschino	karate	Darren
Barrymore	sarcoma	yarmulke	Karl
Newark	Pavarotti	Darjeeling	Charles
Tarheel	Carolyn	Laramie	sardine
Garcia	pearl	Marjory	infarction
Calgary	larynx	Clark	shark

Ending Shape AR

sonar	vinegar	cedar	solar
molar	Vassar	Edgar	bazaar
Caesar	vicar	Babar	spear
Omar	czar	polar	Oscar
nectar	jaguar	registrar	briar
boar	friar	samovar	

Let's Get Personal

➤ **Suggested Activity:** With a partner, share the following information. Answers can be factual or invented. Be sure to use appropriate ASL structure and grammatical features for your answers.

1.   **8 to 5:**
       Your job title?
       Where you eat lunch?
       Your supervisor's name?
       Your e-mail address?

2.   **School Days:**
       Name of your third-grade teacher?
       Name of your first crush?
       What was your high school mascot?
       What was the name of your favorite high school teacher?

3.   **Cars:**
       What was the make and model of your first car?
       What is the make and model of your current car?
       If you could own any car in the world, what would it be?
       What kind of car would you NEVER want to drive?

Getting Creative

➤ **Suggested Activity:** Each student selects one topic from those provided below (22 topics provided), and creates a short story (4 to 5 sentences) that incorporates the elements listed for that topic. Stories can be presented within small groups, or to the entire class.

1. **Race Announcement:**
   Marathon
   Grand Ledge Park
   Gatorade
   First Prize: Schwinn bicycle

2. **Sports Update:**
   NCAA basketball tournament
   MSU Spartans
   Duke Blue Devils
   New Orleans Superdome

3. **News Flash:**
   Protestors riot
   Caesar Chavez Avenue
   National Guard
   Monroe County Hospital

4. **Job Posting:**
   University Bugle Intern
   Features Editor
   McCormack Building
   Faculty Advisor: Xena Zuber

5. **Soccer Program:**
   "Pay to Play" sports
   September-October
   Parks and Recreation
   Contact: Carol Barrow

6. **Girls' Basketball:**
   Maria and Denise
   Lady Thunderbirds
   Springfield High School
   mascot

7. **High School Years:**
   Valedictorian
   Bloomington, Indiana
   Member, Future Farmers of
       America
   National Honor Society

8. **College Life:**
   Ball State University
   Phi Kappa Zeta
   Klinger Hall
   Study Abroad: Munich

9. **Outdoor Fun:**
   Seward Glacier trail
   fleece jacket
   grizzly bear cubs
   Polaroid

10. **Directions:**
    Wayne Highway
    Trapper Creek Exit
    Corner of Newton and Oak
    "Brenda Sue's Diner"

11. **Birthday Girl:**
    August
    angel food cake
    piñata
    Legos

12. **Transportation:**
    Amtrak
    Joliet to Cleveland
    Transfer in Toledo
    Express Route

13. **The 1970s:**
    Disco
    John Travolta
    Bee Gees
    "Saturday Night Fever"

14. **Summertime:**
    Grover Park
    deviled eggs
    mayonnaise
    botulism

Getting Creative (continued)

15. **Mexico:**
Cancun
Paradiso Hotel
tequila
Montezuma's revenge

16. **Shopping:**
Wal-Mart
greeter
Garth Brooks CD
Little Debbie snack cakes

17. **Real Estate:**
Re/Max
condominium
fixer-upper
carport

18. **Dating:**
limo
La Cucina Italian Restaurant
Club Fernando
daiquiris

19. **Personal Ad:**
SWM
soul mate
walks on beach
vegetarian

20. **Luck:**
lottery tickets
convenience store
IRS
Costa Rica

21. **Baseball:**
Chicago Cubs
Wrigley Field
Cracker Jacks
Sammy Sosa

22. **Meditation:**
guru
incense
mantra
yoga

Unit Eight

- ❖ **Warm-Up Exercises**
- ❖ **Developmental Shape Drills**
- ❖ **Acronyms**
- ❖ **Finger Twisters**

Warm-Up Exercises

Shoulder Shrugs: Slowly raise and drop shoulders several times.

The Swan Dive: Slowly stretch arms above your head until they meet, palms together. Gently lower them to shoulder level, palms up. Repeat.

Finger Lifts: Place hand palm down on a table or flat surface and slowly raise and lower each finger. Repeat with the other hand.

Full Arm Stretch: Hold arm out parallel to the floor, palm down. Lock elbow. Raise your hand so the fingertips point to the ceiling. With the other hand, gently press the raised fingers back toward your body, for a five-count. Alternate with the other hand and repeat twice.

Palm Press: Press palms together in front of your body. Keeping your elbows high, use your right palm to gently and slowly push the left palm backwards, from the wrist only, toward the left elbow. Slowly and gently, use the left palm to push the right palm backward, from the wrist only, toward the right elbow. Repeat several times.

The Frankenstein: With arms stretched out in front of you, palms down, slowly open and close hands, stretching the fingers apart as far as possible. Repeat several times.

Wrist Revolutions: With closed hands, slowly rotate wrists in toward each other several times. Then rotate wrists away from each other several times.

Drill Shape RI

ria	ria	rib	ric
Maria	Siberia	Ribera	Rick
Brian	triage	riboflavin	Richard
Brianna	Miriam	cribbage	Ricardo
Adrian	mariachi	scribe	rickets
Adriatic	Rialto	Tribbles	cricket
			Brickhouse

ric	ric	ric	rid
Eric	Zurich	varicose	riddle
Erica	Jericho	fricative	The Riddler
ricotta	Richter	fricassee	Bridget
Ricci	Richmond	trichinosis	Bride of Frankenstein
Gingrich		triceratops	

rie	rif	rig	rig
Marie	Griffin	Rigel	Brighton
Patrie	Griffiths	Rigoletto	Wright
Erie	Brussels griffon	Rigby	Cartwright
brie	grifter	rigatoni	brigade
Ariel	orifice		marigold
Orient			origami
Riesling			

rij	rik	ril	rim
frijoles	Rikki	Rilla	crimson
marijuana	Riki-Tiki-Tavi	krill	Rimini
	Mariko	April	Rimes
	trike	Riley	Crimea
		Marilyn	Grimm
		trilogy	Purim
		Amarillo	

Drill Shape RI (continued)

rin	rin	rio	rip
Erin	Ringo	Rio Grande	Ripley
meringue	ringworm	Orion	riptide
urine	Ringwald	Orioles	tripe
urinal	Rin Tin Tin	Chariots of Fire	Tripoli
latrine	Corrina		
Trina	Slytherin		
Katrina			
Princeton			

riq	ris	ris	ris
briquette	Chris	Iris	risotto
	Christine	Aristotle	Frisbee
	Christina	Aristophanes	prism
	Crispin	Boris	Priscilla
	Kris Kringle	Morris	Trisha
	Rice Krispies	Garrison	Kristi

rit	riu	riv	rix
Magrit	Marius	rivet	Trixie
Rita	Tiberius	trivet	Beatrix
Margarita		trivia	aviatrix
Ritz		The River Wild	dominatrix
Fritz		Rivera	
Fritos		Riverton	
Ritter		Riverside	
Fritter			

riz
grizzly
Rizzo
Fabrizio

Leading Shape PH

Phoenix	Phyllis	Philemon	pheasant
Philippines	phagocyte	phallic	pharmacist
phantom	Phillip	phlegm	phobia
pharynx	Phi Beta Kappa	phosphate	Philco
phylum	Phoebe	phlox	pheromone
phlebotomy	photon	Phelps	Pharisee
Phineas	Phoenicia	phlebitis	Phnom Penh
Pharaoh	photosynthesis	phooey	phantasmagoria
phaser	phylactery	phosphorous	philodendron

Embedded Shape PH

sapphire	Sophie	zephyr	gopher
morpheme	spheroid	Westphall	Euphrates
Stephanie	aphid	Humphrey	Sophocles
hemisphere	typhoon	sophomore	camphor
Christopher	Stephen	sulphur	syphilis
macrophage	Memphis	cellophane	xenophobia
dolphin	Epiphany	Daphne	hieroglyphics
The Prophet	sulphate	calligraphy	cipher
Alphonse	Raphael	chlorophyll	Ephraim
atmosphere	euphemism	encephalic	Iphigenia
Aphrodite	delphinium	schizophrenia	Sappho

Ending Shape PH

Ralph	morph	caliph	nymph
Joseph	graph	Rudolph	ectomorph
endomorph	lymph	staph	

Acronyms

When fingerspelling three-letter acronyms, the first letter is produced with a tight, clockwise circle; the other two letters are produced as standard, linear fingerspelling. This movement differentiates an acronym from a straightforward fingerspelled element.

Practice with the following acronyms:

Federal Bureau of Investigation	FBI
Central Intelligence Agency	CIA
National Theatre of the Deaf	NTD
Very important person	VIP
Americans With Disabilities Act	ADA
Deaf President Now	DPN
World Games for the Deaf	WGD
Unidentified flying object	UFO
Black Deaf Advocates	BDA
Conference of Interpreter Trainers	CIT
Internal Revenue Service	IRS
Tender loving care	TLC

Some acronyms within the Deaf community are so commonly used and recognized, they do not follow the first-letter-circled pattern, but instead are fingerspelled in the standard linear form. These include:

National Association of the Deaf	NAD
Registry of Interpreters for the Deaf	RID
Social Security	SS
Supplemental Security Income	SSI
Supplemental Security Disability Insurance	SSD

Acronyms with four or more letters are produced in a linear fashion. Practice with the following acronyms:

National Technical Institute for the Deaf	NTID
Child of Deaf Adults	CODA
California State University, Northridge	CSUN
American Sign Language Teachers Association	ASLTA
National Fraternal Society of the Deaf	NFSD (a.k.a. FRAT)
National Association for the Advancement of Colored People	NAACP
United States Deaf Bowling Federation	USDBF
American Association of the Deaf-Blind	AADB

Finger Twisters

➤ **Suggested Activity:** With a partner, each of you fold your copy in half lengthwise. Fingerspell a phobia from the phobia list to your partner, who will then fingerspell what the phobia is about.

Phobia:	Fear of:
arachnophobia	spiders
anthropophobia or sociophobia	people and social situations
avaiatophobia or aerophobia	flying
agoraphobia, cemophobia, or kenophobia	open spaces
claustrophobia, cleisiophobia, cleithrophobia, clithrophobia	confined spaces
emetophobia	vomiting
acrophobia, altophobia, hysophobia, or hypsiphobia	heights
brontophobia or keraunophobia	thunderstorms
astraphobia	lightning
lilapsophobia	hurricanes and tornadoes
necrophobia or thanatophiobia	death
ophiophobia	snakes
trypanophobia	injections
phasmophobia	ghosts
bacillphobia	bacteria
zoophobia	animals
neophobia	new things
demonphobia	evil supernatural things

▶ Unit Nine

- ❖ **Warm-Up Exercises**
- ❖ **Developmental Shape Drills**
- ❖ **Business Cards**
- ❖ **Alphabet Questions**
- ❖ **Half and Half**

Warm-Up Exercises

Shoulder Shrugs: Slowly raise and drop shoulders several times.

The Swan Dive: Slowly stretch arms above your head until they meet, palms together. Gently lower them to shoulder level, palms up. Repeat.

Finger Lifts: Place hand palm down on a table or flat surface and slowly raise and lower each finger. Repeat with the other hand.

Full Arm Stretch: Hold arm out parallel to the floor, palm down. Lock elbow. Raise your hand so the fingertips point to the ceiling. With the other hand, gently press the raised fingers back toward your body, for a five-count. Alternate with the other hand and repeat twice.

Palm Press: Press palms together in front of your body. Keeping your elbows high, use your right palm to gently and slowly push the left palm backwards, from the wrist only, toward the left elbow. Slowly and gently, use the left palm to push the right palm backward, from the wrist only, toward the right elbow. Repeat several times.

The Frankenstein: With arms stretched out in front of you, palms down, slowly open and close hands, stretching the fingers apart as far as possible. Repeat several times.

Wrist Revolutions: With closed hands, slowly rotate wrists in toward each other several times. Then rotate wrists away from each other several times.

Drill Shape AR

aar	bar	car	car
AARP	Barry	Carol	carnation
Aaron	Barrymore	Carolyn	caramel
bazaar	Ibarra	Carl	caribou
	Babar	Carla	carcinoma
	Barbara	Carlson	Oscar
	rubarb	Carter	Scarlett
	Barcelona	Carey	Scarpeti
	baroque	Carney	Scaramouche
		Coscarelli	scarab

dar	ear	far	gar
Darren	Earl	Farr	Gary
Darlene	pearl	Farrell	Calgary
Daryl	Spears	Fargo	Garrison
Darjeeling	Pearce	Farmer	Garrett
Darkwing Duck	Meara	Farley	garnet
Cedar Point	Meares	infarction	Garth
			Niagara Falls

gar	har	har	jar
Garcia	Harry	Harpo	Jared
garlic	Harrison	Harvard	Jarrett
gardenia	Charles	harlequin	Jar-Jar Binks
garbanzo	Charleston	Sahara	
vinegar	Charlene	shark	
Edgar	Sharon	Phar Lap	
	Sharpe	pharynx	

kar	lar	lar	mar
Karen	Larry	Laramie	Mark
karate	lark	larynx	Marx
Jakarta	Larkin	Abelard	Marie
Karl	Clark	flare	Marvin
Karla	Clarke	solar	Martin
Kareem	Lara	molar	Omar
	Clara	polar	Nomar
	Laredo	Polaroid	

Drill Shape AR (continued)

mar	nar	par	rar
maraschino	sonar	Parr	Ferarri
marquis	Gunnar	Park	Girardi
veal marsala	narcolepsy	South Park	registrar
Maris	narwhal	Parker	
Marius		Spartans	
Marjory		Spartacus	
Maryvonne		Parcheesi	
		parasite	

sar	tar	uar	var
Sarah	Tarzan	Stuart	LeVar
Sarajevo	Tarheel	jaguar	Varney
sardine	Starr	quart	ovary
sarcoma	Starkey	quarantine	varicose
Caesar	nectar		samovar
Vassar	notary		Pavarotti
			Shevardnadze

war	xar	yar	zar
Ward	Pixar	Yarnell	Zara
warden		yarmulke	czar
Warren			czarina
wart			
Stewart			
Hogwarts			
Newark			
Dewars			

Leading Shape RO

royal	rocket	Robert	Rover
Roxy	Robyn	robin	Romeo
rodeo	Rotterdam	Roquefort	Roxanne
Romania	rogue	rostrum	Rocker
Rome	roadrunner	Roger	rouge
Roget	Roanoke	Robbins	Rochelle
rococo	roulette	Rockefeller	Rockne
Rodin	Roland	rosary	Rousseau
romaine	Roosevelt	Roswell	Roth
Rosa	roux	roseola	Rowena
Rouen	rosemary	Rossetti	rotunda
Roth	roundworm	roughage	rosary
Roswell	rosacea	robot	Rodman
Rolaids	Rogaine	Rome	rotting

Embedded Shape RO

dromedary	broccoli	Troy	irony
Detroit	peroxide	Turrow	drone
Proust	kangaroo	Brock	crocodile
carob	Gilroy	Conroy	Sharon
Globetrotters	Strom	tropical	Cromwell
Petrov	baroque	Prozac	arrow
Monroe	strobe	android	troll
Harold	Gross	groin	crow
broil	crock	proctor	bronze
barrow	chrome	Grover	Tyrone
Ambrose	grouse	fibroblast	Farrow
Troilus	introit	grommet	propeller
troglodyte	Peron	coroner	Melrose
Carolyn	Frodo	Croft	Kudrow
Broadway	Aykroyd	trolley	steroid
saffron	Tootsie Roll	chromosome	Harold
Cameron	Farouk	macaroon	

Ending Shape RO

burro	Euro	taro	Shapiro
Karo	Sbarro	Ichiro	Nero
faro	Spiro	Navarro	Hasbro
Hillsboro	sombrero	macro	Pedro
Cicero	gyro	Renfro	milagro
Charo	Astro	tyro	Jethro

Business Cards

➤ **Suggested Activity:** Using the "business cards" below (collect your own, as well), practice the following: first names, last names, company names, titles, street and city names, and proper ASL state signs and abbreviations.

THE HUBCAP SOURCE
Jacob Sisko, CEO
4923 Walnut Street
New Brunswick, Vermont 97450

MIDAS MUFFLER SHOP
Zachary Hillman, Manager
8847 W. Parish Drive
Saugatuck, Louisiana 44729

KENT COUNTY SHERIFF'S DEPT
Edith Zuber, Sheriff
684 Calvison Avenue
Livonia, Mississippi 48720

THE ARC OF ST. LOUIS
Betty Anne Rowe, Director
5862 Arca Drive
St. Louis, Arkansas 96807

UNIVERSITY OF SOUTH DAKOTA
Sheri Swain, Student Union Coordinator
Jim Thorpe Building
311 Campus Center Drive
Providence, South Dakota 47621

DATELINE NBC
Ina Jaffe, Associate Producer
42 Rockefeller Plaza
Albany, New York 10012

U.S. THREADS, SCRUBS AND UNIFORMS
Avery M. Wayne, Sales & Marketing Manager
321 Baker Street
Kalkaska, Wyoming 48726

BAVARIAN BRATS AND BEER
Greta Graholm, Proprietor
7301 Schooner Way
Sudsbury, Pennsylvania 35491

TIFFANY COLLECTIONS
Steve King
2908 Rodeo Drive
Burbank, Maine 03101

PERSONAL DESIGN GROUP
Deb Bradley, Consultant
1929 Market Place
Omaha, New Jersey 21831

KENNETH L. PURDUE
Orthopedic Surgeon
2815 N. Cavanaugh Way
Tallahassee, Kentucky 55948

SERENITY SALON
Lillian Belsky, Massage Therapist
3525 Jefferson Street
Phoenix, Nebraska 74029

OFFICE OF CIVIL RIGHTS
Ashley Wright, Lead Investigator
189 Lois Lane
Honolulu, North Dakota 99652

TOTAL IMAGE SPA
Maddy Kloeckener, Stylist
6203 Vineyard Boulevard
Topeka, North Carolina 38344

CHEZ ANTOINE
Luc Bessier, Sommelier
105 Ryan Place
Paris, Oregon 87950

MARY KAY COSMETICS
Cindy Bakker, Sales Representative
8210 Carnation Avenue
Pinksdale, Texas 72003

Alphabet Questions

➤ **Suggested Activity:** In pairs, students create, ask, and respond to questions in which the question and answer key word is fingerspelled following the letters of the alphabet.

Examples:

Student 1:   SUPPOSE ME LIVE-THERE <u>A</u>RGENTINA, MY JOB WHAT?
Student 2:   YOUR JOB <u>A</u>STRONOMER

Student 2:   SUPPOSE MYSELF ANIMAL <u>B</u>ABOON, ME EAT WHAT?
Student 1:   YOU EAT <u>B</u>READFRUIT

Student 1:   SUPPOSE ME COOK <u>C</u>HOWDER NEED PUT-IN WHAT?
Student 2:   PUT-IN <u>C</u>LAM NEED

Half and Half

➤ **Suggested Activity:** Divide into pairs, with one person taking List A, and the other taking List B. The person with List A chooses at random one of the commonly known pairs from the list, and fingerspells the first half to the partner. The partner responds by fingerspelling the word that completes the pair. (Some pairs may have acceptable matches other than the ones listed.) When an appropriate match has been given, the exercise alternates, and the person with List B gives the first half of a pair.

List A	List B
Abercrombie and Fitch	liver and onions
Pat Sajak and Vanna White	Santa and Mrs. Claus
Proctor and Gamble	Democrats and Republicans
Dorothy and Toto	Yin and Yang
Lone Ranger and Tonto	wine and cheese
Tweedledee and Tweedledum	push and pull
Sherlock Holmes and Dr. Watson	pro and con
Thelma and Louise	Snoopy and Charlie Brown
bagels and lox	masculine and feminine
Hansel and Gretel	arts and crafts
Romeo and Juliet	Bert and Ernie
Tarzan and Jane	pen and pencil
Barbie and Ken	Bedknobs and Broomsticks
Wile E. Coyote and the Roadrunner	Bonnie and Clyde
Mickey and Minnie	peanut butter and jelly
Better Homes and Gardens	shampoo and conditioner
Jack and the Beanstalk	Raggedy Ann and Andy
Dr. Jekyll and Mr. Hyde	Mork and Mindy
green eggs and ham	John Lennon and Yoko Ono
R2D2 and C3PO	latitude and longitude

▶ Unit Ten

- ❖ **Warm-Up Exercises**
- ❖ **Developmental Shape Drills**
- ❖ **Advertising Slogans**
- ❖ **Categories**
- ❖ **Let's Get Personal**

Warm-Up Exercises

Shoulder Shrugs: Slowly raise and drop shoulders several times.

The Swan Dive: Slowly stretch arms above your head until they meet, palms together. Gently lower them to shoulder level, palms up. Repeat.

Finger Lifts: Place hand palm down on a table or flat surface and slowly raise and lower each finger. Repeat with the other hand.

Full Arm Stretch: Hold arm out parallel to the floor, palm down. Lock elbow. Raise your hand so the fingertips point to the ceiling. With the other hand, gently press the raised fingers back toward your body, for a five-count. Alternate with the other hand and repeat twice.

Palm Press: Press palms together in front of your body. Keeping your elbows high, use your right palm to gently and slowly push the left palm backwards, from the wrist only, toward the left elbow. Slowly and gently, use the left palm to push the right palm backward, from the wrist only, toward the right elbow. Repeat several times.

The Frankenstein: With arms stretched out in front of you, palms down, slowly open and close hands, stretching the fingers apart as far as possible. Repeat several times.

Wrist Revolutions: With closed hands, slowly rotate wrists in toward each other several times. Then rotate wrists away from each other several times.

Drill Shape UN

aun	bun	cun	dun
faun	bunt	cuneiform	dung
fauna	bundt	Cancun	dune
sauna	Bunche	fecund	Dunne
La Shaundra	bungalow		dungeon
	Bunsen		Dungeness
	Bunyan		Duncan
	cummerbund		Dunston
	Bundy		
	Bunker Hill		
fun	gun	hun	jun
funnel	Gunnar	shunt	Cajun
defunct	Gunga Din	Hunter	June
fungi	Gunther	Huntsville	Jung
fungus	Gunnison	Huntley	Juneau
fundus	gunnysack	Bethune	juniper
fungo	Gund	Chunnel	junta
Funt	Gundam		Junction City
lun	mun	nun	oun
lunar	Munster	Nunn	noun
Lunden	Munson	nunchuck	Pound
spelunker	Munich	nuncio	Norton Sound
	Edmund	conundrum	Rounders
	Muncie		
	Munising		
	immunity		
	Munroe		
pun	run	sun	tun
punt	Runser	Sung	tundra
pundit	Runyan	Sun Yat-Sen	tuna
Punic	Runnymede	sundae	tungsten
Punjab	rune	sundries	tunic
Punxsutawney	prune	Gunderson	Tunis
Punky Brewster	brunch	SUNY	Tunisia
	Bull Run		Tunney
			stun gun

Leading Shape RI

Richard	Riley	Ricci	rigatoni
Rimini	ricotta	riboflavin	Richmond
Rigel	ringworm	Rio Grande	Rialto
Rick	Rigoletto	Ripley	Riverside
Ribera	Richter	riptide	rivet
Ricardo	Riesling	Riverton	Rita
Ritter	ritz	risotto	Richelieu
rickets	riddle	rime	Rin Tin Tin
The Riddler	Rivera	The River Wild	Ringo

Embedded Shape RI

triage	Eric	Iris	Jericho
Morris	cribbage	brie	Brian
urinal	cricket	Frisbee	tripe
Orioles	triceratops	trivia	frijoles
briquette	orifice	Ariel	grizzly
Maria	Aristotle	Crimea	laterine
Purim	meringue	Princeton	Fritz
marijuana	Zurich	fricative	Trisha
Marilyn	origami	fritter	Orient
prism	Trixie	varicose	aviatrix
marigold	trivet	urine	mariachi
Boris	Grimm	Garrison	Wright
Erin	Erie	Tripoli	trike
fricassee	brigade	trilogy	Orion
Aristophanes	Crispin	trichinosis	Marius

Ending Shape RI

Shari	Kari	Lori	harikari
safari	Tori	beriberi	Yuri
sari	Jeri	Cori	Teri
Henri	Mata Hari		

Advertising Slogans

➤ **Suggested Activity:** With partners, one student fingerspells a slogan from column A while the other student responds with the matching product or company from column B. (See Answer Key, page 110, in Appendix B.)

Column A

"Have It Your Way"

"Finger Lickin' Good!"

"We Love to See You Smile"

"Do the Dew"

"Melts in Your Mouth, Not in Your Hand"

"Where's The Beef?"

"Let Your Fingers Do the Walking"

"Good to the Last Drop"

"Got Milk?"

"You're in Good Hands"

"When It Rains, It Pours"

"Just Say No"

"The Other White Meat"

"Don't Leave Home Without It"

"Just Do It"

"We'll Leave the Lights on for You"

"It's the Real Thing"

"Snap! Crackle! Pop!"

"They're Grrrrrrreat!"

"Take the Plunge"

"Mmm, Mmmm Good!"

"The Breakfast of Champions"

"Bet You Can't Eat Just One"

Column B

American Express

Coca-Cola

The National Council on Pork

Yellow Pages

Nestea

Morton Salt

Frosted Flakes

M & Ms

Burger King

Wendy's

The American Dairy Council

Motel 6

The War on Drugs

Maxwell House

Lay's Potato Chips

Wheaties

Campbell's Soup

Allstate

Nike

McDonald's

Kentucky Fried Chicken

Rice Krispies

Mountain Dew

Categories

➤ **Suggested Activity:** With a partner or in small groups, fingerspell items that belong to the following categories. (For some sample answers, see the Answer Key, page 111, in Appendix B.)

Walt Disney Movies

_____	_____	_____
_____	_____	_____
_____	_____	_____
_____	_____	_____
_____	_____	_____
_____	_____	_____
_____	_____	_____
_____		

United States Presidents

_____	_____	_____
_____	_____	_____
_____	_____	_____
_____	_____	_____
_____	_____	_____
_____	_____	_____
_____	_____	_____
_____	_____	_____
_____	_____	_____
_____	_____	_____
_____		

Breeds of Dogs

_____	_____	_____
_____	_____	_____
_____	_____	_____
_____	_____	_____
_____	_____	_____
_____	_____	_____
_____	_____	_____
_____	_____	_____
_____	_____	_____
_____		

Let's Get Personal

➤ **Suggested Activity:** With a partner, share the following information. Answers can be factual or invented. Be sure to use appropriate ASL structure and grammatical features for your answers.

1. **About You:**
   What brand of toothpaste do you use?
   What do you take for a headache?
   What soft drink do you drink most often?
   What store do you shop in the most?

2. **Hobby:**
   What hobbies do you have?
   What was the last homemade Christmas present you gave?
   Where do you buy supplies for your hobby?
   Where do you read about or exchange information regarding your hobby?

3. **Dream Vacation:**
   Where would you go?
   Who would you take along?
   What sites/attractions would you see?
   What would you eat?

Unit Eleven

- ❖ **Warm-Up Exercises**
- ❖ **Developmental Shape Drills**
- ❖ **Categories**
- ❖ **In What Order?**

Warm-Up Exercises

Shoulder Shrugs: Slowly raise and drop shoulders several times.

The Swan Dive: Slowly stretch arms above your head until they meet, palms together. Gently lower them to shoulder level, palms up. Repeat.

Finger Lifts: Place hand palm down on a table or flat surface and slowly raise and lower each finger. Repeat with the other hand.

Full Arm Stretch: Hold arm out parallel to the floor, palm down. Lock elbow. Raise your hand so the fingertips point to the ceiling. With the other hand, gently press the raised fingers back toward your body, for a five-count. Alternate with the other hand and repeat twice.

Palm Press: Press palms together in front of your body. Keeping your elbows high, use your right palm to gently and slowly push the left palm backwards, from the wrist only, toward the left elbow. Slowly and gently, use the left palm to push the right palm backward, from the wrist only, toward the right elbow. Repeat several times.

The Frankenstein: With arms stretched out in front of you, palms down, slowly open and close hands, stretching the fingers apart as far as possible. Repeat several times.

Wrist Revolutions: With closed hands, slowly rotate wrists in toward each other several times. Then rotate wrists away from each other several times.

Drill Shape OM

bom	com	com	dom
bomb	coma	compost	Domino's
Bombay	sarcoma	Compton	Dominique
bombardier	glaucoma	Compazine	Dominican
Albom	comet	Wycombe	Dominus
gom	hom	hom	kom
Gomez	hominy	Homer	Komodo dragon
Gomer	homily	Homerville	Komura
Gompers	homburg	Homestead	Komondor
Gomorrah		Thomas	
lom	mom	nom	nom
Loman	Mombassa	Nome	astronomy
Salome	Momence	nomad	gastronomy
Shalom	Momus	ignominy	carcinoma
Lombard			
Lombardy			
Golom			
oom	pom	pom	rom
Rosenbloom	pomander	Pomp	Rome
oomiak	pomegranate	Pompeii	chrome
oomph	Pomeroy	Pompidou	chromosome
doom			Romney
Coomer			Romper Room
loom			
rom	rom	rom	som
Romania	Cromwell	Prometheus	insomnia
Romanov	Cro Magnon	Romulus	sommelier
Romney	Strom	thrombosis	Somalia
Romano	Romero	Tromso	Somerset
			Somoza
tom	wom	yom	zom
atom	wombat	Yom Kippur	zombie
anatomy		Wyoming	
stoma			
phantom			
Tommy			

Leading Shape EL

Elaine	Elba	Elden	Electra
Elias	Elbert	elderberry	electrolytes
Elam	Elbertson	El Dorado	eleemosynary
eland	El Cajon	Eldridge	element
elastic	El Capitan	Eleanor	Elena
elephantiasis	elf	Elgin	El Greco
elixir	elk	Elk Horn	Ellen
Ellington	elm	Elmhurst	Elmira
El Paso	Elroy	Elsa	El Salvador
Elsinore	eluvium	Elvira	Elvis
Ely	Elyria		

Embedded Shape EL

Disraeli	Velveteen Rabbit	Tel Aviv	Celt
Melinda	Velcro	Belmont	Wellington
Telemundo	Helga	Melrose Park	pelican
Lewellyn	Yeltsin	Delmonico	relish
Welk	helium	Wellesley	cello
Welsh	Alka-Seltzer	Belle	Spielberg
Zelig	jelly bean	Feldman	Yellowstone
Melmac	Rumsfeld	Lela	Nellie
Delilah	Helms	Bellingham	Melvin
Helena	cellophane	Cruella	spelunker
Nelson	helix	pelvis	feldspar
Dell	Melissa	Belize	velour
Helsinki	Zelda	Felipe	veld
Celeste	Skelton	mazel tov	gelatin
Selznick	Felicity	Melville	Jell-O
delphinium	Delhi	beluga	Rondell
Shelley	shillelagh	belladonna	Nellis
Johnny Belinda	Kelsey	celery	Felix
Daniels	Kellogg	Heller	Belgrade

Ending Shape EL

Israel	Handel	Nigel	Tufnel
Mabel	Hufnagel	glockenspiel	fennel
Babel	kennel	Tarheel	falafel
Siskel	Chunnel	shrapnel	Noel
Morel	Hansel	Denzel	mohel
Captain Marvel	Carmel	Ariel	Hummel

Categories

➤ **Suggested Activity:** With a partner or in small groups, fingerspell items that belong to the following categories. (For some sample answers, see the Answer Key, page 112, in Appendix B.)

Stephen King Novels

_____	_____	_____
_____	_____	_____
_____	_____	_____
_____	_____	_____
_____	_____	_____
_____	_____	_____
_____	_____	

Types of Tea

_____	_____	_____
_____	_____	_____
_____	_____	_____
_____	_____	_____
_____	_____	_____
_____	_____	

Soap Operas

_____	_____	_____
_____	_____	_____
_____	_____	_____
_____	_____	_____
_____	_____	

In What Order?

➤ **Suggested Activity:** Instructor fingerspells the words in each group in random order, one at a time. After each word, students must correctly identify the word, and write the number corresponding to the order in which the instructor fingerspelled it next to the word.

_____ Liza	_____ Belinda	_____ polar
_____ Eliza	_____ Bermuda	_____ solar
_____ lizard	_____ Beluga	_____ molar
_____ blizzard	_____ Bologna	_____ sonar

_____ Diane	_____ harp	_____ Helen
_____ Diana	_____ Harpo	_____ Helena
_____ Dinah	_____ sharp	_____ Heller
_____ Dyane	_____ Sharpe	_____ Helper
	_____ Shemp	_____ Hedda

_____ Kenneth	_____ rang	_____ Mary
_____ Kenner	_____ range	_____ Marie
_____ Dennis	_____ ranger	_____ Maria
_____ Denise	_____ Granger	_____ Maris
_____ Donner	_____ orange	_____ Marlis

▶ Unit Twelve

- ❖ **Warm-Up Exercises**
- ❖ **Developmental Shape Drills**
- ❖ **Categories**
- ❖ **Words Per Minute**
- ❖ **Visual Discrimination**

Warm-Up Exercises

Shoulder Shrugs: Slowly raise and drop shoulders several times.

The Swan Dive: Slowly stretch arms above your head until they meet, palms together. Gently lower them to shoulder level, palms up. Repeat.

Finger Lifts: Place hand palm down on a table or flat surface and slowly raise and lower each finger. Repeat with the other hand.

Full Arm Stretch: Hold arm out parallel to the floor, palm down. Lock elbow. Raise your hand so the fingertips point to the ceiling. With the other hand, gently press the raised fingers back toward your body, for a five-count. Alternate with the other hand and repeat twice.

Palm Press: Press palms together in front of your body. Keeping your elbows high, use your right palm to gently and slowly push the left palm backwards, from the wrist only, toward the left elbow. Slowly and gently, use the left palm to push the right palm backward, from the wrist only, toward the right elbow. Repeat several times.

The Frankenstein: With arms stretched out in front of you, palms down, slowly open and close hands, stretching the fingers apart as far as possible. Repeat several times.

Wrist Revolutions: With closed hands, slowly rotate wrists in toward each other several times. Then rotate wrists away from each other several times.

Drill shape PH

aph	eph	iph	lph
Aphrodite	Stephen	siphon	dolphin
aphid	Stephanie	cipher	sulphur
graph	Joseph	biphenyl	sulphate
geography	Ephriam	caliph	Ralph
calligraphy	encephalic	Epiphany	Rudolph
staph	zephyr	Iphigenia	Alphonse
Daphne			delphinium
Raphael			

mph	oph	oph	pph
lymph	Sophie	cellophane	sapphire
nymph	Sophia	macrophage	Sappho
Memphis	Sophocles	xenophobia	
camphor	sophomore	The Prophet	
Humphrey	Christopher	chlorophyll	
Pumphrey	gopher	schizophrenia	
symphony			

rph	sph	tph	uph
morph	spheroid	Westphall	euphoria
endomorph	atmosphere		Euphrates
ectomorph	hemisphere		euphemism
morphology			
morpheme			

yph
syphilis
typhoon
hieroglyphics

Leading Shape OM

omelet	omen	Omaha	O'Malley
Oman	omega	omniscient	ombudsman
Omar	omnivore	omentum	omicron
omphaloskepsis	Omsk	Omuta	omnibus

Embedded Shape OM

Yom Kippur	Bombay	Thunderdome	Cromwell
Tommy	Lombard	comet	trombone
anatomy	astronomy	gastronomy	thrombosis
chrome	Gomorrah	Pompeii	wombat
Mombassa	Gomez	Comanche	Lipscomb
Nome	Domino's	commodore	Salome
Rome	Romulus	Pompey	Commodus
Tom Collins	Compazine	Cro Magnon	infomercial
Pomeranian	Komodo dragon	Homer	Prometheus
Comstock	oomph	hominy	Dominican
sarcoma	carcinoma	chromosome	homeopathy
zombie	insomnia	sommelier	Como
aromatherapy	Loch Lomand	Compton	Silverdome
communist	Loman	Momence	glaucoma
Thomas	bombardier	Dominique	homburg
Gomer	pomegranate	romaine	Romeo
Romero	Somoza	Pompidou	Gompers
Broomhilda	endometriosis	nomad	oomiak
Komura	Dominus	Somaliland	Pomona
Somerset	Tomlinson	compost	Homestead

Ending Shape OM

Folsom	dot-com	idiom	Epsom
Rosenbloom	atom	phantom	Strom
Albom	shalom	slalom	prom
Golom	doom	loom	

Categories

➤ **Suggested Activity:** With a partner or in small groups, fingerspell items that belong to the following categories. (For some sample answers, see the Answer Key, page 113, in Appendix B.)

Baseball Teams

_____	_____	_____
_____	_____	_____
_____	_____	_____
_____	_____	_____
_____	_____	_____
_____	_____	_____
_____	_____	_____
_____	_____	_____

String Instruments

_____	_____	_____
_____	_____	_____
_____	_____	_____
_____	_____	

Types of Cheese

_____	_____	_____
_____	_____	_____
_____	_____	_____
_____	_____	_____
_____	_____	_____
_____	_____	_____

Words Per Minute

➤ **Suggested Activity:** Divide into pairs. One person holds the following list at eye level for the other. When the instructor gives a signal, the person not holding the list begins to fingerspell the words on the list. Each word must be fingerspelled clearly and completely (the person holding the list acts as an "accountability judge," ensuring each word is fingerspelled clearly and completely). At the end of one minute, the instructor gives a stop signal. Count how many words were fingerspelled, switch roles, and repeat.

Compare to your previous Words Per Minute in Unit Four.

1.	RUN	21.	WITTY
2.	FUN	22.	CON
3.	BUN	23.	DON
4.	GUN	24.	NON
5.	NUN	25.	SON
6.	PUN	26.	TON
7.	SUN	27.	WON
8.	FUNNY	28.	CONE
9.	RUNNY	29.	DONE
10.	BUNNY	30.	NONE
11.	SUNNY	31.	TONE
12.	YOUNG	32.	GONE
13.	FIT	33.	HONE
14.	HIT	34.	LONE
15.	KIT	35.	DOG
16.	PIT	36.	FOG
17.	SIT	37.	HOG
18.	WIT	38.	JOG
19.	KITTY	39.	LOG
20.	PITY	40.	NOG

Visual Discrimination

➤ **Suggested Activities:**

1. The student receives the list. The instructor fingerspells one of each pair, and the student must circle the correct one.

2. The words below are copied onto index cards, and the students play "Go Fish."

Alcott	Phoenix	begonia
Abbott	Alex	Patagonia
drizzle	Marilyn	Dirk
dazzle	Marlin	Dick
Fuller	bowel	Brady
Miller	Howell	Brandy
Minneapolis	Tolstoy	Rachel
Indianapolis	Tokyo	Richard
Clifton	quota	Godzilla
Lipton	aqua	gorilla
Denise	Esther	cashew
Dennis	Heather	Shaw
Mack	Frank	maple
Mark	Hank	Marple
Sally	tundra	Anne
Molly	tuna	Anna
Stewart	tango	Phillip
Seward	Congo	Phyllis
Gary	Julie	blister
Harry	Julia	bluster
rugby	tart	Panama
Rigby	tort	Pomona
Bali	Dixie	Mervin
Dali	Dixon	Marvin
fennel	herpes	Newman
funnel	gherkins	Newton
jest	clout	Donny
zest	trout	Denny

Visual Discrimination (continued)

asthma	halitosis	parasite
Athena	hypnosis	paradise
Mary	enamel	Jerry
Emily	camel	jelly
allergy	copper	Foxx
allegory	Cooper	Fixx
Lewis	Eddie	toffee
kiwis	Effie	noodle
Anastasia	warts	pinna
euthanasia	tarts	penne
Timmy	Mike	Dana
Tommy	Nike	Diana
Bronson	John	tarantella
Branson	Jan	tarantula
Janice	pepperoni	Ruby
Joyce	paparazzi	Rudy
Libby	convex	Mickey
Liddy	cortex	Nicky
Perry	Dean	Monet
Terry	Liam	Manet
Duncan	minaret	lava
Dunstan	minuet	larva
Taylor	Jean	asterisk
Tyler	Joan	asteroid
vowel	Ellis	Danny
bowel	Eddie	Donny
Potter	Katrina	guru
Peter	Sabrina	Peru

Appendix A

Manual Alphabet Illustration

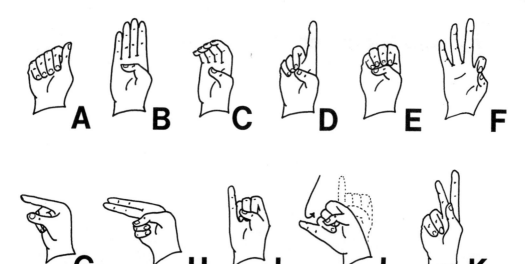

A B C D E F

 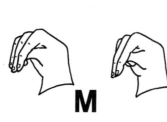 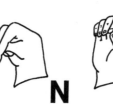 

G H I J K

 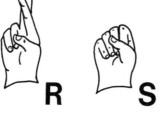  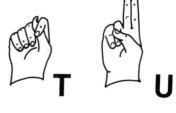

L M N O P

  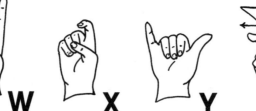 

Q R S T U

V W X Y Z

Appendix B

Answer Keys

Unit Two Answer Key: Seeing Shapes

1. A **lion** is king of the jungle.

2. The **tiger**, also of the cat family, is found in India.

3. An **elephant** has a prehensile trunk.

4. A **snake** dislocates its jaw to swallow prey.

5. A **monkey** is adept at swinging from branches.

6. A grizzly **bear** hibernates in winter.

7. Take the groceries to the **kitchen**.

8. Put candles on the table in the **dining room**.

9. I bought bunk beds for the **bedroom**.

10. The **attic** was infested with squirrels.

11. The **basement** was converted into a rec room.

12. We have a big screen TV in the **living room**.

Unit Three Answer Key: Making Clozure

QUSIMDO **Quasimodo**	RCHL **Rachel**	LZBTH **Elizabeth**
BCTRA **Bacteria**	KLMZO **Kalamazoo**	LINGNI **Linguini**
SPRGTN **Springtown**	FLGFF **Flagstaff**	PNICLN **Penicillin**
CDRLLA **Cinderella**	CLTN **Clinton**	TMTHY **Timothy**
TZMNA **Tazmania**	MLBRNE **Melbourne**	HNRY **Henry**
LXNTN **Lexington**	BFLO **Buffalo**	SHKSPR **Shakespeare**
CHYNE **Cheyenne**	JRY **Jerry**	ZBR **Zebra**
LZRD **Lizard**	AMRLLO **Amarillo**	ANDRSN **Anderson**
CPNHGN **Copenhagen**	BJNG **Beijing**	SWZKPF **Schwarzkopf**
PTLND **Portland**	JSCA **Jessica**	DNLD **Donald**
CRWFD **Crawford**	BKWRM **Bookworm**	CRLYN **Carolyn**
OLV GRDN **Olive Garden**	JC PNY **JC Penney**	CLVLND **Cleveland**
BNJMN **Benjamin**	DFODL **Daffodil**	BSTN **Boston**
MRGRT **Margaret**	DTH VDR **Darth Vader**	HLYWD **Hollywood**
SPRGFLD **Springfield**	HNKKH **Hanukkah**	LTHUNA **Lithuania**
RKFLR **Rockefeller**	STPHN **Stephen**	TSCNY **Tuscany**
LVRPL **Liverpool**	NDLPNT **Needlepoint**	MCHL **Michael**
BRBRA **Barbara**	PNSTTA **Poinsettia**	NW ZLND **New Zealand**

Unit Three Answer Key: Geography Bowl

1. Which state is known as "The Last Frontier?"
   Alaska

2. Name the five (5) Great Lakes.
   Huron, Ontario, Michigan, Erie, Superior

3. Name seven (7) states that border the Atlantic Ocean
   Maine, New Hampshire, Massachusetts, Rhode Island, Connecticut, New York, New Jersey, Delaware, Maryland, Virginia, North Carolina, South Carolina, Georgia, Florida

4. Name three (3) states that border the Pacific Ocean.
   Alaska, Hawaii, Washington, Oregon, California

5. Which two (2) mountain states are shaped like squares?
   Colorado and Wyoming

6. Which four (4) states border Mexico?
   California, Arizona, New Mexico, Texas

7. Name five (5) states that border Canada.
   Alaska, Washington, Idaho, Montana, North Dakota, Minnesota, Michigan, New York, Vermont, New Hampshire, Maine, Wisconsin, Ohio, Pennsylvania

8. Which state is located on both the Gulf of Mexico and the Atlantic Ocean?
   Florida

9. Name three (3) of the Hawaiian Islands.
   Hawaii, Maui, Oahu, Kauai, Lanai, Nihau, Kahoolawe, Molokai

10. Which state is shaped like a boot?
    Louisiana

11. Which state is surrounded by freshwater lakes?
    Michigan

12. What is the capital of Indiana?
    Indianapolis

13. Name four (4) of the seven states that border Kentucky.
    Illinois, Indiana, Ohio, West Virginia, Virginia, Tennessee, Missouri

14. What state is known as "the Cornhusker State"?
    Nebraska

15. Name three (3) of the four state capitals with the word "City" in their names.
    Oklahoma City, Oklahoma, Carson City, Nevada, Jefferson City, Missouri, Salt Lake City, Utah

Unit Four Answer Key: Making Clozure with Context

1. To make a rich spaghetti sauce, you need tomatoes and plenty of RGNO.
   OREGANO

2. The results of my biopsy showed the tumor to be BNGN.
   BENIGN

3. My favorite Christmas candle scent is MLBRY.
   MULBERRY

4. Amanda's favorite Disney movie is LTL MRMD.
   LITTLE MERMAID

5. Tristan sent college applications to DRMT PRCTN YLE.
   DARTMOUTH   PRINCETON   YALE

6. For the French Club's final meeting, we ate at CHZ LUIS. I just had the French onion soup, but Lydia tried the ESCRGT.
   CHEZ LOUIS   ESCARGOT

7. When I was in Rome, I saw several works by MCLNGLO including the STNE CHPL ceiling, and the PITA.
   MICHELANGELO   SISTINE CHAPEL   PIETA

8. In Paris, I saw the GRGYL at Notre Dame and the FFL Tower.
   GARGOYLES   EIFFEL

9. Stephen King wrote one of my favorite books, GRN ML. It was made into a movie with TM HKS.
   GREEN MILE   TOM HANKS

10. When we go out to eat, Jeff orders a PTRHSE steak. I usually order the FLT MGN.
    PORTERHOUSE   FILET MIGNON

11. Because Susan was afraid her boyfriend would become violent when they broke up, she got a RSTRNG RDR against him.
    RESTRAINING ORDER

12. Bailey's favorite characters on Sesame Street are SCR and BG BRD.
    OSCAR   BIG BIRD

13. At the amusement park, Terry and Cathy rode three rides, the RLR CSTR the MRY G RND and the TLT WRL.
    ROLLER COASTER   MERRY-GO-ROUND   TILT-A-WHIRL

Unit Four Answer Key:
Making Clozure with Context (continued)

14. Chris decided to become a flight attendant for STHWST Airlines and moved to TCSN.
    SOUTHWEST   TUCSON

15. Because local doctors couldn't figure out what was wrong with her, Marie was sent first to the MYO CLNC, and then to the JHN HPKNS Medical Center.
    MAYO CLINIC   JOHNS HOPKINS

16. Our third president, Thomas JFRSN, lived at MNTCLO, in Virginia.
    JEFFERSON   MONTICELLO

17. When our dental HYGNST had a baby, we gave her a gift certificate to TRGT.
    HYGIENIST   TARGET

Unit Five Answer Key: ASL Abbreviations

States	**Abbreviations**
Alabama	ALA
Connecticut	CONN
Delaware	DEL
Florida	FLA
Georgia	GA
Illinois	ILL
Indiana	IND
Kentucky	KY
Maine	MAINE
Maryland	MD
Massachusetts	MASS
Michigan	MICH
Mississippi	MISS
New Hampshire	NH
New Jersey	NJ
New York	NY
North Carolina	NC
Ohio	OHIO
Pennsylvania	PA or PENN
Rhode Island	RI
South Carolina	SC
Tennessee	TENN
Vermont	VT
Virginia	VA
West Virginia	West VA
Wisconsin	WISC

Unit Ten Answer Key: Advertising Slogans

Column A	Column B
"Have It Your Way"	Burger King
"Finger Lickin' Good!"	Kentucky Fried Chicken
"We Love to See You Smile"	McDonald's
"Do the Dew"	Mountain Dew
"Melts in Your Mouth, Not in Your Hand"	M & Ms
"Where's The Beef?"	Wendy's
"Let Your Fingers Do the Walking"	Yellow Pages
"Good to the Last Drop"	Maxwell House
"Got Milk?"	The American Dairy Council
"You're in Good Hands"	Allstate
"When It Rains, It Pours"	Morton Salt
"Just Say No"	The War on Drugs
"The Other White Meat"	The National Council on Pork
"Don't Leave Home Without It"	American Express
"Just Do It"	Nike
"We'll Leave the Lights on for You"	Motel 6
"It's the Real Thing"	Coca-Cola
"Snap! Crackle! Pop!"	Rice Krispies
"They're Grrrrrrreat!"	Frosted Flakes
"Take the Plunge"	Nestea
"Mmm, Mmmm Good!"	Campbell's Soup
"The Breakfast of Champions"	Wheaties
"Bet You Can't Eat Just One"	Lay's Potato Chips

Unit Ten Answer Key: Categories

Walt Disney Movies

Aladdin
Alice in Wonderland
Beauty and the Beast
Bedknobs and Broomsticks
Cinderella
Dumbo
The Hunchback of Notre Dame
The Jungle Book

Lady and the Tramp
Little Mermaid
The Love Bug
Mary Poppins
Mulan
Peter Pan
Pete's Dragon
Pinocchio

Pocahontas
The Rescuers
Snow White & the Seven Dwarfs
Tarzan
Toy Story
Winnie the Pooh
101 Dalmatians

United States Presidents

John Adams
John Quincy Adams
Chester Arthur
James Buchanan
George H.W. Bush
George W. Bush
Jimmy Carter
Grover Cleveland
William Clinton
Dwight D. Eisenhower
Gerald Ford
James Garfield

Ulysses S. Grant
Warren G. Harding
William H. Harrison
Rutherford B. Hayes
Herbert Hoover
Andrew Jackson
Thomas Jefferson
Lyndon B. Johnson
John F. Kennedy
Abraham Lincoln
James Madison
Franklin Pierce

James Polk
Ronald Reagan
Franklin Roosevelt
Theodore Roosevelt
William Taft
Zachary Taylor
Harry S. Truman
Martin Van Buren
George Washington
Woodrow Wilson

Breeds of Dogs

Afghan
Akita
Basset Hound
Beagle
Bichon Frise
Bloodhound
Borzoi
Boxer
Bulldog
Chihuahua
Chow Chow

Collie
Cocker Spaniel
Dachshund
Dalmatian
German Shepard
Great Dane
Greyhound
Golden Retriever
Husky
Labrador
Lhasa Apso

Pekingese
Poodle
Rottweiler
Shih Tzu
Springer
Terrier
Welsh Gorgi
Whippet
Wolfhound

Unit Eleven Answer Key: Categories

Stephen King Novels

Bag of Bones
Carrie
Christine
Cujo
Dead Zone
Desperation
Dolores Claiborne
Dreamcatcher
Firestarter

Gerald's Game
The Girl Who Loved Tom Gordon
The Green Mile
Hearts in Atlantis
It
Misery
Needful Things
Night Shift
Pet Sematary

Riding the Bullet
Rose Madder
The Shining

Types of Tea

Chai
Cinnamon Stick
Constant Comment
Darjeeling
Earl Grey
English Breakfast

Green
Iced
Irish Breakfast
Lady Grey
Lapsong Souchong
Lemon Lift

Lipton
Mint
Orange Pekoe
Orange Spice
Oolong
Prince of Whales

Soap Operas

All My Children
Another World
As the World Turns
The Bold and the Beautiful
Days of Our Lives

General Hospital
Guiding Light
One Life to Live
Passions
Peyton Place

Port Charles
Santa Barbara
Search for Tomorrow
The Young and the Restless

Unit Twelve Answer Key: Categories

Baseball Teams

Angels	Expos	Reds
Astros	Giants	Red Sox
Athletics	Indians	Rockies
Blue Jays	Mariners	Royals
Braves	Marlins	Tigers
Brewers	Mets	Twins
Cardinals	Orioles	White Sox
Cubs	Padres	Yankees
Devil Rays	Pirates	
Diamondbacks	Phillies	
Dodgers	Rangers	

String Instruments

banjo	harp	sitar
bass	lute	viola
cello	lyre	violin
dulcimer	mandolin	zither
guitar	shamisen	

Types of Cheese

American	gouda	parmesan
bleu	havarti	provolone
Brie	jalapeno	romano
cheddar	limburger	string
feta	Monterey Jack	Swiss
goat	mozzarella	velveeta

Appendix C

More Suggested Activities

Relay Race

Instructor divides the class into teams. One person from each team goes to the blackboard, ready to write. The instructor fingerspells a word. The first student to correctly write the word on the board wins a point for his or her team. Play to 10 or 15 points.

tweed	taxi	poker	century
cramps	brandy	stripe	sparkle
riddle	Globetrotter	kangaroo	Prozac
trapeze	rodeo	asteroid	chess
frijoles	omelet	bagel	jaguar
celery	jellyfish	hostel	daffodil
garlic	penicillin	enema	estrogen
goldfish	grizzly	Fritos	broccoli
baboon	atom	bomb	bazaar
tattoo	gnat	latte	buzzer
coleslaw	scampi	sesame	sword
Ellen	Allen	Danny	Donny

City, State and Country Relay Race

Instructor divides the class into teams. One person from each team goes to the blackboard, ready to write. The instructor fingerspells a name of a city, state, or country, either from the following list or from an instructor-created list. The first student to correctly write the word on the board wins a point for his or her team. Play to 10 or 15 points.

Anchorage	Orlando	Trenton
Denver	Bloomington	Annapolis
Rome	Belize	Hagerstown
Belgium	Romania	Bangor
Oregon	Utah	Salem
Wyoming	Halifax	Syracuse
Arabia	Babylon	Burlington
Copenhagen	Melbourne	Concord
Sudan	Tel Aviv	Schenectady
El Paso	Iceland	Scranton
Jericho	Athens	Pensacola
Vienna	Eugene	Hot Springs
Phoenix	Greenland	Greensboro
Aspen	Lexington	Mobile
Richmond	Zurich	Shreveport
Brooklyn	Sioux Falls	Biloxi
San Jose	Dominican Republic	Knoxville
Barcelona	Calgary	Paducah
Hong Kong	Sarajevo	Lubbock
Newark	Liechtenstein	Roswell
Baton Rouge	Argentina	Yuma
Honolulu	Makapala	Enid
Branson	Winnemucca	Duluth
Kenya	Mozambique	Wichita
Beijing	Bangkok	Ogallala
Sri Lanka	Afghanistan	Davenport
Moscow	Lithuania	Rockford
Warsaw	Wittenberg	Marquette
Madrid	Dublin	Akron
Havana	San Juan	Bozeman
Guadalajara	Halifax	Elko
Saskatchewan	Pocatello	Durango
Peoria	Oshkosh	Laramie
Toledo	Bismarck	Provo
Des Moines	Muskogee	Oxnard
Port Arthur	Natchez	Portland
Savannah	Norfolk	Yakima
Wheeling	Reading	Fairbanks

How Many Words?

Single Scribe

Divide the class into two teams. Each team appoints a scribe. Instructor writes a long word on the board, and team members fingerspell words that can be made from that word to the scribe. These can be any words, not just those that would be fingerspelled in American Sign Language. The team with the most words after five minutes wins.

Scribe Switch

Divide the class into two teams. Each team forms a line. Instructor writes a long word on the board. The person at the head of the line is the first receiver/scribe. The second person in the line must fingerspell a word that can be made from the letters in the long word. Scribe records it, and moves to the back of the line. The second person moves up to the receiver/scribe position, and the next person in line fingerspells a word made from the target word. Team with most words after 10 minutes wins.

Variations:

> **Easy**
> Three letter words are accepted.
>
> **Intermediate**
> All words must be at least four letters.
>
> **Challenger**
> All words must be at least five letters.
>
> **Stimulus word suggestions:**
> transportation
> literature
> tranquilizer
> misconception
> calendar
> development
> renaissance
> apothecary
> fingerspelling
> transformation
> arbitration
> nonbiodegradable

Two-Word Relay Race

Instructor divides the class into teams. One person from each team goes to the blackboard, ready to write. The instructor fingerspells a two-word phrase or name either from the following list or from an instructor-created list. The first student to correctly write the word on the board wins a point for his or her team. Play to 10 or 15 points.

Mickey Mouse	tin can
iceberg lettuce	mad cow
Haagen Dasz	wet paint
Agent Orange	Rice Krispies
Bull Run	Tootsie Rolls
Raggedy Ann	jelly bean
chop suey	Alka-Seltzer
pork chops	Mardi Gras
bare feet	Spice Girls
Last Supper	Ice Capades
jet lag	Feng Shui
Groundhog Day	Three Stooges
Underground Railway	Komodo dragon
Universal Studios	Star Wars
Herbert Hoover	Genghis Kahn
Grand Canyon	Boris Yeltsin
Randy Travis	Magic Marker
Ford Mustang	rocky road
turn signal	Taco Bell

ABC Adjectives

Instructor writes an ASL noun phrase on the board. Students take turns each creating a sentence by fingerspelling an adjective following alphabetical order.

Example:

CAR-THERE

<u>a</u>ncient	<u>h</u>	<u>o</u>	<u>v</u>
<u>b</u>attered	<u>i</u>	<u>p</u>	<u>w</u>
<u>c</u>lassy	<u>j</u>	<u>q</u>	<u>x</u>
<u>d</u>usty	<u>k</u>	<u>r</u>	<u>y</u>
<u>e</u>	<u>l</u>	<u>s</u>	z
<u>f</u>	<u>m</u>	<u>t</u>	
g	<u>n</u>	<u>u</u>	

BOY-HE

<u>a</u>ntsy	<u>h</u>	<u>o</u>	<u>v</u>
<u>b</u>rilliant	<u>i</u>	<u>p</u>	<u>w</u>
<u>c</u>ranky	<u>j</u>	<u>q</u>	<u>x</u>
<u>d</u>evoted	<u>k</u>	<u>r</u>	<u>y</u>
<u>e</u>	<u>l</u>	<u>s</u>	z
<u>f</u>	<u>m</u>	<u>t</u>	
g	<u>n</u>	<u>u</u>	

CAFETERIA-IT

<u>a</u>ffordable	<u>h</u>	<u>o</u>	<u>v</u>
<u>b</u>leh!	<u>i</u>	<u>p</u>	<u>w</u>
<u>c</u>heap	<u>j</u>	<u>q</u>	<u>x</u>
<u>d</u>ingy	<u>k</u>	<u>r</u>	<u>y</u>
<u>e</u>	<u>l</u>	<u>s</u>	z
<u>f</u>	<u>m</u>	<u>t</u>	
g	<u>n</u>	<u>u</u>	

Telephone Game

Divide into equal groups and form lines. The first person in each line faces the instructor; the rest turn their backs. The instructor fingerspells, one time only, one of the following phrases to the front row of students. Those students then turn, tap the next ones in line, and fingerspell to them the same phrase, one time only. The process continues through the line, until the last person has seen the phrase. That person comes to the front of the line and fingerspells the phrase back to the instructor. Teams with the correct phrase score one point for their team. Play to 5 points.

Chevy Cavalier	Mall of America
Kraft Macaroni and Cheese	Goldfish crackers
Christopher Columbus	Grandfather clock
antibacterial soap	American Red Cross
extracurricular activities	Backstreet Boys
skunk cabbage	Hertz Rent-A-Car
digital TV	gingerbread house
super-information highway	McDonald's Quarter Pounder
Hair Club for Men	Los Angeles Coliseum
cellular telephone	"Bride of Frankenstein"
Microsoft Windows	continuing education units
Ask Jeeves	Chattanooga, Tennessee
New York Stock Exchange	Chihuahua puppies
"The Brady Bunch"	"Gone With the Wind"
rhubarb pie	Fenway Park
Alice Cogswell	"Star Spangled Banner"
Bugs Bunny	"Little Miss Muffet"

Commercial Board Game Adaptations

Many commercial board games can be adapted for fingerspelling practice, including Jeopardy! and Wheel of Fortune. Here are some others:

Junior Trivial Pursuit: Sign the questions and answers in ASL with a partner, incorporating fingerspelled and numeric information.

Memory Madness: Cards with category topics (Famous Lawyers, Bridges, Condiments, Shades of Green, etc.).
Uses:
- One person knows the topic and fingerspells items that fit the category until the category is guessed.
- All but one person knows the category and group members fingerspell category items to that person until s/he guesses the category.
- Everyone knows the category and items are fingerspelled around the group until the list is exhausted.
- As an evaluation tool; instructor fingerspells five items related to the category and students must identify category (means student can miss an item, and still get the category).

Scattagories: Similar to Memory Madness. Categories include Pizza Toppings, Kinds of Candy, Things with Tails, Things in a Medicine Cabinet.

Scrabble: Students can pull 3-4 tiles, and must fingerspell words containing those letters.

Taboo: Fingerspell the "forbidden" clues listed on the card to get partner to identify the target word.

Relay Race

Instructor divides the class into teams. One person from each team goes to the blackboard, ready to write. The instructor fingerspells a word (either from the following list or from an instructor-created list). The first student to correctly write the word on the board wins a point for his or her team. Play to 10 or 15 points.

pirate	liver
camel	maze
pilgrim	gravity
bagpipes	estrogen
season	diabetes
pumice	rigatoni
marijuana	marigold
ringworm	robot
wheat	Elvis Presley
coleslaw	compost
grasshopper	argyle
goldfish	prune
blackberry	Guatemala
yeast	oyster
galaxy	dragon
hospice	orangutan
glossary	Yabba Dabba Doo
urban	centipede
valet	kiwi fruit
brass	sardine
scarf	armadillo
pimple	Aladdin
lime	Fruit Loops
what	Holiday Inn
job	Dr. Seuss
bank	Archie Bunker
early	Red Lobster
style	sauerkraut

To The Letter

Divide into groups of three. One person is the moderator; the other two are the players. The moderator chooses any letter of the alphabet. Players must alternate fingerspelling words that begin with that letter, and would be fingerspelled in American Sign Language. The first player who is unable to come up with a word, repeats an already used word, or uses a word that would not normally be fingerspelled in ASL loses the round, and a point is awarded to the other player.

Play continues by switching roles, to allow each person turns as the moderator. The first person to reach 5 points wins.

Display and Describe

(The Grown-Up Version of Show and Tell)

Students prepare a 3-5 minute presentation on something: a hobby, a picture from a vacation, a pet, a favorite book or movie, etc. The presentation should be in ASL, with appropriately incorporated fingerspelled elements.

▶ Bibliography and Resource List

Bahleda, S. (1996). *Fingerspelling the real world*. Eagle River, AK: Real World Press.

Battison, R. (1978). *Lexical borrowing in American Sign Language*. Silver Spring, MD: Linstock Press.

Fingerspelling and numbers [computer software]. (1994). Salem, OR: Sign Enhancers, Inc.

Fingerspelling geographic locations [videotape]. (1991). Burtonsville, MD: Sign Media, Inc.

Fingerspelled loan signs [videotape]. (1991). Burtonsville, MD: Sign Media, Inc.

Fingerspelling miscellaneous items [videotape]. (1991). Burtonsville, MD. Sign Media, Inc.

Fingerspelling proper names [videotape]. (1991). Burtonsville, MD: Sign Media, Inc.

Groode, J. (1992). *Fingerspelling: Expressive and receptive fluency* [videotape]. San Diego, CA: Dawn Sign Press.

Interactive sign language fingerspelling and numbers [computer software]. (1997). Seattle, WA: Palatine, Inc.

Lane, H. (1984). *When the mind hears: A history of the deaf*. New York: Random House.

Patrie, C. (1997). *Fingerspelled names and introductions: A template building approach* [videotape]. San Diego, CA: Dawn Sign Press.

Schein, J. (1984). *Speaking the language of sign: The art and science of signing*. New York: Doubleday.

Stewart, D., Schein, J., & Cartwright, B. (1998). *Sign language interpreting: Exploring its art and science*. Needham Heights, MA: Allyn and Bacon.

Notes